ETTY
HILLESUM

MODERN SPIRITUAL MASTERS
Robert Ellsberg, Series Editor

This series introduces the writing and vision of some of the great spiritual masters of the twentieth century. Along with selections from their writings, each volume includes a comprehensive introduction, presenting the author's life and writings in context and drawing attention to points of special relevance to contemporary spirituality.

Some of these authors found a wide audience in their lifetimes. In other cases recognition has come long after their deaths. Some are rooted in long-established traditions of spirituality. Others charted new, untested paths. In each case, however, the authors in this series have engaged in a spiritual journey shaped by the influences and concerns of our age. Such concerns include the challenges of modern science, religious pluralism, secularism, and the quest for social justice.

At the dawn of a new millennium this series commends these modern spiritual masters, along with the saints and witnesses of previous centuries, as guides and companions to a new generation of seekers.

ETTY HILLESUM

Essential Writings

Selected with an Introduction by

ANNEMARIE S. KIDDER

ORBIS BOOKS

Maryknoll, New York 10545

Library of Congress Cataloging-in-Publication Data

Hillesum, Etty, 1914–1943.
    [Selections. English. 2009]
    Etty Hillesum : essential writings / selected with an introduction by Annemarie S. Kidder.
       p. cm. – (Modern spiritual masters)
      ISBN 978-1-57075-838-6 (pbk.)
      1. Hillesum, Etty, 1914–1943. 2. Holocaust, Jewish (1939–1945) – Netherlands – Personal narratives. 3. Jews – Netherlands – Biography. 4. Netherlands – Ethnic relations. I. Kidder, Annemarie S. II. Title. III. Title: Essential writings.
    DS135.N6H5478 2009
    940.53′18092 – dc22
    [B]

                                      2009012061

To Margaret Brennan, IHM,
and the IHM sisters of Monroe, Michigan,
whose lives and ministries have mirrored to me
the spirit of Etty

Contents

Introduction

In recent years, a young Jewish woman from the Netherlands has gained worldwide acclaim for her writings. Considered "a singular hero" of the Nazi era — whose victim she became — she has emerged through her writings as a mystic who, amid the war's horrors, could affirm the goodness and beauty of life, and as a spiritual master who taught herself, as she teaches others, to explore the landscape of the soul and the soul's quest for truth and God. Her diaries, covering a two-year period (1941–42), were first published in 1981 in Dutch and in 1983 in English. Chronicling in nuanced detail and with brilliant literary skill the gradual spiritual transformation she experienced, they have received the attention of psychologists, literary critics, historians of the Holocaust, scholars in women's studies, spiritual directors, and theologians. With the publication of her diaries and letters into more than a dozen languages and with the appearance in 2002 of a comprehensive, annotated English edition, many questions remain: Who was the woman whose once troubled and restless soul came to exude an inner peace and a joie de vivre that was contagious, and still is? What prompted the change of attitude and perception in her and what were the intellectual, spiritual, and social forces that served as incubator and catalyst? And what can she teach contemporary seekers of wisdom about the life of the spirit, the mysterious encounter with God, the attainment of a heartfelt conviction that life is beautiful and good, even in the most dismal and disheartening circumstances? To be sure, she knew such circumstances. For many months, at her request, she agreed to live at a cramped transit camp: She wished to be with her fellow Dutch Jews in order to dispense, like medicine, words of kindness and acts of mercy, while each week more than a thousand of them, frightened children and adults, were being transported to a Polish concentration camp. On September 7, 1943, she and her family were placed on the train as well. Near the tracks, someone found a postcard she had tossed from a window, which read, "We left the camp singing.... Good-bye for now from the four of us." She died in Auschwitz on November 30, 1943, at the age of twenty-nine.

A Short Life

Today, this young woman's diaries and letters, written between 1941 and 1943, constitute an important historical witness to the suffering of Jews and non-Jews during the era of the Holocaust and the Nazi occupation. As such, they have become a critical piece of Jewish national and cultural history and of its heritage in the Netherlands. Their survival is largely due to the author herself, who at one time considered discarding her diaries for the "schoolgirlish nonsense" they contained but then decided to keep them, less for their potential historical value to future generations than for the chronicle they contained of her spiritual transformation. The name of their author is Esther "Etty" Hillesum (1914–43), henceforth referred to as "Etty," which is the name by which she addressed herself throughout her diary entries and with which she signed her letters.

What do we know about her? Apart from the information gleaned through the two-year window of her diaries and letters, we know little about her background and prior life. Born on January 15, 1914, in Middelburg to Dutch Jewish parents, Etty was the eldest of three children; her brother Jaap was two years younger and her brother Mischa six. Her father, Louis, was a teacher of classical languages at various gymnasiums (grammar schools), first in Middelburg, then in Hilversum and Tiel. In 1918, the family moved to Winschoten so the father could accept a position there as headmaster and teacher of classics. In 1924 he was appointed to a similar position at the gymnasium in Deventer, where he became headmaster in 1928 and was among the community's leading citizens. Her mother, Riva, was born and raised in Russia and had come to the Netherlands as the result of a pogrom. Her profession at the time was recorded as Russian-language teacher, and she and Louis were married in 1912. Although conscious of their Jewish identity, the Hillesum family probably did not regularly observe Jewish religious practices and though Etty regarded herself as religious, she acknowledges that the posture of prayer and kneeling she came to adopt for herself was "not handed down from generation to generation with us Jews." We know that her father worked on Saturdays, but it is uncertain whether the family otherwise attended synagogue and celebrated Jewish festivals.

Cultural interests and activities permeated the Hillesum household, including the reading of classical literature, musical performance, and language studies in Hebrew, Greek, French, Russian, and German. All three children graduated from gymnasium. Etty pursued studies at the University of Amsterdam both in law and in Slavic languages and literature, earning a master's degree in law in 1939. Jaap studied medicine at the University of Amsterdam and later at Leiden to become a physician. And Mischa, whose striking musical talent at a very young age won him a national reputation, went on to study piano. However, the family atmosphere was also beset by internal turmoil, temperamental volatility, and strife. To Etty, her family was "a remarkable mixture of barbarism and culture." Most members struggled with some kind of nervous condition, psychological illness, and bouts of depression. Their mother had suffered numerous nervous breakdowns, Jaap was committed to

psychiatric hospitals on several occasions, and Mischa underwent treatments for schizophrenia. Only their father seems to
have been exempt from the family malaise. Etty, also, fought
with periods of inner fragmentation, depression, and immobility,
sleeping for long stretches at a time, experimenting with self-
medication, and experiencing moments of physical and internal
fatigue and extreme mood swings. It was on account of these
symptoms and behavioral patterns that she welcomed the introduction to a renowned German psychoanalyst and chirologist
who had moved his practice from Berlin to Amsterdam and who
agreed to take her on as a patient.

Meeting Julius Spier (1887–42) proved a critical, life-changing
event for Etty and set in motion a spiritual yearning for inner
transformation and tranquility. After meeting Spier on February 3, 1941, the day on which by her own account her soul was
born and "I was brought into the world," a deep friendship developed. Within a short time Etty had become Spier's assistant and
confidante. To her, he was "the mediator between God and me,"
a skilled discerner of the divine within humans, a seeker of God
and a finder of God in every human heart that would open up
to him. Spier was born in Frankfurt am Main to Jewish parents,
the sixth of seven children. At age fourteen, he had entered an
apprenticeship at the Beer Sontheimer trading company, working
his way up to a management position. While his former dream had
been to become a singer, a dream foiled by a hearing impairment,
he continued to move in artistic circles. In addition to setting up
his own publishing house, he took an interest in chirology, the
study of reading palms. After twenty-five years with the trading
firm, he left the business in 1926 to study psychoanalysis with
Carl Gustav Jung in Zurich. After two years of study and at
Jung's suggestion, Spier opened a practice of psycho-chirology
in Berlin. The practice was highly successful and Spier's reputation spread quickly. He gave public lectures and courses in the
field in Switzerland, Germany, and the Netherlands, along with

demonstrations in clinics and psychiatric institutions. Following his divorce from his wife of seventeen years, he became engaged to his pupil Hertha Levi. Due to the uncertain situation for Jews in Nazi Germany, Levi emigrated to London in 1937 or 1938, while Spier emigrated to Amsterdam in 1939. At first living with his sister, Spier rented two rooms from a family from late 1940 on, where he set up practice and taught courses. The students at those courses would invite "models," whose hands Spier would then analyze by way of practical demonstration. Etty had been invited by one of her housemates to serve as Spier's "model."

It was probably at Spier's recommendation and as part of her therapy that Etty began writing a journal, or "exercise book." Recording her thoughts allowed her to monitor the dynamic landscape of her soul and to practice an inner listening, or a *hineinhorchen* into the soul, an activity for which she could find no proper Dutch word. The close listening to the soul revealed her inner ambiguities and conflicting feelings, while permitting her to practice a blunt honesty with herself as well as a gentleness and concern for her soul's well-being. "Etty, my girl, I am not at all pleased with you," she would say chidingly. Then would follow a heart-to-heart talk with herself about why she was displeased, an analysis of her faulty thinking or her flights of fancy, and a lively and tenacious search for how best to clear up things within — a search that would often result in her copying out longer passages from books on psychology, philosophy, and poetry, along with wisdom sayings and scriptural quotations. Many of her diary entries close with a cheerful parting greeting, a "good night now!" as if to signal a tender patience with herself, a spirit willing to reconcile the contending factions within her, and the confidence that things would turn out right after all and perhaps become much clearer to her the next day. In addition to the therapeutic effects that diary writing had on her, Etty hoped that it would provide her with future material for a novel. Among various topics, she toyed with the idea of writing a novel about "the girl who could not kneel" — a reference to her personal struggle with daily prayer, a practice that she knew Spier observed and that she fervently wished to emulate.

The influence of Spier on Etty's spiritual development can hardly be overestimated. He not only taught her to come to terms with her depressive moods, her egocentricities, and her self-absorption, but also helped her practice mental and spiritual hygiene. To that end, he introduced her to the Bible and the writings of St. Augustine, probably the *Confessions,* along with those of his former mentor, C. G. Jung and various Christian writers and mystics. From the age of twelve, Etty had been reading widely, including the works by the Russian writer Fjodor Dostoevsky and those of other Russian poets and novelists. She also was familiar with the German-language poet Rainer Maria Rilke, who had sought to serve as a bridge between East and West, Russia and continental Europe, and with whose writings and the role of the artist as bridge-builder she could readily identify. Under Spier's tutelage, however, these writers' works took on a deeper meaning, one that would transform her outlook on life, on God, on her fellow human beings.

Spier's therapeutic approach included unusual measures. He invited his clients to participate in wrestling matches with him designed to bring body and spirit into proper balance. He also encouraged physical contact within bounds, such as touching and caressing, which invariably generated erotic responses and romantic notions among his mostly female clientele. Presumably, such physical stimulation would prompt people to try to restore balance by engaging their mental and spiritual capacities and becoming more inclined to seek assistance from within, from their inner center or core. Despite their unconventionality, Spier's therapeutic measures seem to have borne remarkable results, facilitating among clients the ability to become attuned to the body and giving them greater awareness of and increased autonomy in connecting with their soul. Etty's diaries speak repeatedly and in great detail about her need of having to regroup, detach, and spiritually ground herself after daily contact and telephone conversations with Spier. They also speak of the effort it took her to shed her erotic ambitions and the longing to possess Spier as "my one man," and the agony of practicing such detachment and centering. In that, she is somewhat assisted by Spier's resolve to follow "his chastity plan" and remain emotionally and sexually faithful and committed to his fiancée, Hertha, in London and by the fact that Etty herself was already in an intimate relationship with the widowed accountant Hendrik "Han" Wegerif, who, more than twice her age, had hired her as his live-in housekeeper. Despite their mutual and tender affection and spiritual kinship, a certain distance prevailed in the student-teacher, disciple-master relationship of Etty and Spier. Separated as far as living quarters went by "three streets, a canal, and a little bridge," they found it appropriate until near the end of their friendship to use the cordial German "Sie" in addressing each other, rather than the familiar "Du."

The Writings

At her desk in Amsterdam, Etty continued writing her diaries, or "exercise books," until three months after she had begun work at the transit camp for Dutch Jews at Westerbork, the Netherlands. This became possible because during these three months, she regularly traveled back to Amsterdam. A total of ten notebooks have survived, with the seventh missing and possibly the very first one also, along with the one she kept at Westerbork, which she took with her on the train to Auschwitz. The extant diaries begin on March 8, 1941, one month after her meeting Spier, and end on October 13, 1942, overlapping with her work at Westerbork that had begun on July 30, 1942.

Due to a gallbladder infection followed by hospitalization but no surgery, Etty was forced to remain in Amsterdam between December 5, 1942, and June 5, 1943, in order to recuperate. She was dismayed by the slow recovery and yearned to resume her work at Westerbork as soon as possible.

Sometime in May or early June 1943 but prior to her June 6 departure for Westerbork, she gave the Amsterdam diaries, which she called "a silly piece of writing," to Maria Tuinzing, who was then living in the same house as Etty. At the time, Etty may have realized that her intermittent returns to Amsterdam would become less frequent or would cease altogether. Of Tuinzing she requested that the diaries, contained in spiral notebooks, be passed on to the writer Klaas Smelik and that they be published in case she should not return. In 1946 or 1947, Tuinzing turned over the exercise books and a bundle of letters to Klaas Smelik and his daughter Johanna. "Jopie" Smelik then typed out sections. However, Smelik's attempts to have the diaries published during the 1950s and 1960s proved fruitless. Only two of Etty's letters, sent from Westerbork, appeared in a 1943 illegal edition of a work that purported to contain letters written by a Dutch painter, Johannes Baptiste van der Pluym (1843–1912), in order to camouflage the book's true contents.

In 1979, Klaas A. D. Smelik approached the publisher Jan G. Gaarlandt with the request to publish Etty's diaries left to him by his father. This resulted in the 1981 Dutch publication of the diaries, titled *An Interrupted Life*, the 1982 Dutch publication of her letters, titled *The Thinking Heart of the Barracks*, and the 1986 Dutch combined edition of all of her known writings at the time, both diaries and letters. Both diaries and letters were first published in English in 1996 and in an expanded and annotated edition in 2002. The 2002 English edition, from which the current excerpts are taken, contains many more letters: a total of seventy-one dated letters, thirty-three of which were written from Amsterdam during her periods of leave, the others from Westerbork, along with several letters written to her and about her, and three newly found and undated letters of hers. Etty's letters date from between August 5, 1941, and September 7, 1943, the last one scribbled on the postcard she had thrown from the freight train on which she, her parents, and brother Mischa were being deported to Auschwitz. None of them survived.

A New Beginning

In reading the body of Etty Hillesum's work, both diaries and letters, one can discern a distinct turning point, a watershed in her interior life, a break with her former self. This break occurs in Exercise Book Ten, sometime in the middle of July 1942, and marks her awareness of the growing anti-Jewish measures of the Nazi regime. Even though Etty is determined to pursue her own spiritual development and fortify her inner ground and center, the reports of cruelty against Jews, rumors of their mass execution, and the increasingly difficult conditions marked by food shortages, curfews, the confiscation of property, and their ban from public places and establishments could no longer be ignored by her. It is at this point that her spiritual insights nurtured in the isolated cell of her interior, her ideas and her experiences with the state of her soul, the spiritual disciplines of prayer and Scripture reading, and the wisdom of spiritual writers absorbed and accumulated up until then were being put to the test for their practical worth. In her growing autonomy and independence from Spier's influence and an increased reliance on her own intimate relationship with God, Etty is abruptly confronted with the realities of war and her responsibility to become socially active and involved. This call to action came when her name was commended "for some sort of soft job with the Jewish Council."

The Jewish Council was an organization coopted by the German Nazi regime to help transport Jews out of the country. Etty was conflicted about the possibility of working for the Council, aware that it was "a hotbed of intrigue" and that "resentment against this strange agency" was growing "by the hour," since by it "one section of the Jewish population is helping to transport the majority out of the country." Nevertheless, she submitted her resume, and when the position of typist was offered to her at the Amsterdam office of the Council on July 15, she accepted it in hopes that her presence there might allow for some good to come of it. When a few weeks later the Council was in need of workers at the transit camp at Westerbork, Etty volunteered to be sent there, even though this would mean living on the campsite and in an environment of cramped and noisy quarters, hospital and prison barracks, deprivation and food shortages, illness and lack of hygiene, and in the constant company of death. With her application to the department of "Social Welfare for People in Transit" at Westerbork, she was transferred there on July 30, 1942. It was at the camp that her practices of prayer and listening for the presence of God in herself and others would make her "the thinking heart of the barracks." Her connectedness with what was best in her, with God, allowed her to feel connected with everything and everyone there. Her inner attitude and disposition to make herself available to the experience of suffering at the camp permitted her to become an embodied presence of compassion, dispensing simple words and gestures of consolation and love here, a cheerful smile and attentive ear there, and it allowed her to be what her last diary entry says, "willing to act as a balm for all wounds."

The long periods of intense and concentrated listening for the "inner voice" against the backdrop of silence and solitude had produced in Etty considerable autonomy. This autonomy also found expression in the way she was able to cope with the death of the most important person in her life, Julius Spier. When after prolonged suffering from lung disease Spier died on September 15, 1942, Etty had gained enough spiritual maturity to cope with his death with a certain ease, while also realizing that death was to be preferred to the fate that would have awaited him as a Jew.

People, Places, and Themes in the Diaries and Letters

The themes of Etty's diary entries and letters are intertwined with her daily activities and the people with whom she came in close contact. These activities revolve largely around two circles and locations, the Spier group of five devotees and associates and the "family" of five with whom she lived in the same house at 6 Gabriel Metsustraat. The owner of the house was Han Wegerif, who had hired Etty as a housekeeper and to whom she refers as Father Han or Pa Han; his son Hans; a German cook named Käthe Fransen; and two boarders, a chemistry student named Bernard Meijlink and the nurse Maria Tuinzing. Etty's room on the third floor overlooked the main square of Amsterdam, the Museumplein, with the Concert Hall at one end, the Rijksmuseum at the other, and a skating rink in between. The tree outside her window and the sky and stars glimpsed between its branches are frequently mentioned by her as symbols of the unwavering joyous presence of life and life's unity within a vast cosmic expanse.

The second circle is the group of women around Spier, whom Etty had met for the first time on February 3, 1941, the day she called her "birthday." This circle included Adri Holm, Henny "Tide" Tideman, Dicky de Jonge, Liesl Levie, and Etty, who all frequently gathered at Spier's place at 27 Courbetstraat, the house of the Nethe family from whom Spier had rented rooms. Amidst conversations about psychology and palm prints, Spier also served as therapist to each of them. Members of the group also gathered with others for social and musical events, such as regular soirées at friends' homes where Etty's brother Mischa might play the piano and Spier would sing.

Etty's tasks as housekeeper to Wegerif and assistant to Spier were performed with an occasional reluctance. The "family" was in general agreement that Etty's talents lay not in the areas of domestic service, and with this she fully concurred. She considered herself much better suited for helping with Spier's practice by answering correspondence, typing up interview sessions, summarizing patients' diary entries, and copying and editing Spier's lecture notes. But even here she felt at times unfit for the task, stymied, and overwhelmed. The one activity that seemed to suit her well was giving lessons in Russian grammar and Russian literature. Her own Russian language professor had recommended her and sent her students, whom she taught at her home in private lessons which provided her with additional income. Whenever time allowed, she would delight in making translation exercises from Russian into German by searching for just the right word in her Langenscheidt dictionary, scrutinizing her Russian grammar book, and reading the works of Russian authors and poets by comparing the original with its translation. In fact, disciplining herself to regularly make translations became part of what she considered her duty and calling, and she continued the practice even when at Camp Westerbork. It was a way of forgetting herself by means of the patient attention to detail, which, paradoxically, also allowed her to find herself in some ways and to gain a sense of harmony between the interior and exterior worlds.

With her instinctual quest for discerning her true passion and vocation, Etty ended up discovering also the deepest and best inside her, which she called "God." This search and quest gradually led her from first wanting to be a writer and novelist, then a chirologist in Russia (so as to carry on Spier's work in the country of her mother's origin) or a teacher of Russian studies, to eventually desiring to become a cultural mediator between East and West, an artist who united people by offering them the experience of life's beauty, a poet frugal with words and speaking only the necessary against the backdrop of silence to help others shape their "fate from within," a dispenser of love and teacher of God. In the poet Rainer Maria Rilke, Etty found the desires for her own calling affirmed, mirrored, and modeled. It is his work, especially his *Letters to a Young Poet* and *The Book of Hours*, that she quotes throughout her diaries and that suggests frequent themes in her spiritual development.

If for Etty the most important "book" to "read" had been Spier, whose virtues she had sought to appropriate in her own life, now the writings and the wisdom of Rilke would increasingly take on that role. This is not surprising given that, to her, both men were similar: they each "have a large dose of femininity" without ceasing to be "real men" and "they are signposts to the soul." Moreover, both men shared the same language, German. As Spier did not speak Dutch, he and Etty conversed in German, a language that was (and still is) taught in the secondary schools in the Netherlands. Etty read Rilke's writings in the original German, and she recorded all prose and poetry quotations in her diaries and letters in that language as well. Many of the existential themes that Rilke addressed are found in Etty's diaries. However far from merely copying or taking over these themes, she interpreted them in her own refreshingly honest and often humorous manner, demonstrating her striking intellectual capabilities, her keen sense of observation regarding her peers and the political and social conditions around her, and a passionate desire to be "true to myself," to attain a sense of inner harmony and peace amid the distressing outer turmoil. Early on she recognized these ideas' value, taking note of their weight and potential applicability to her own life, but also the fact that she still needed to live into their truth, "like clothes that are much too big and into which I still have to grow."

While the philosophical and spiritual themes in Etty's writings reflect those of Rilke, they are appropriated by her in a manner that is deeply personal and intimately her own. Each theme she carefully tests, meticulously scrutinizes, and repeatedly gauges against her personal life experience. In time, these ideas begin traveling from her head to her heart, or they become like clothes into which she is beginning to grow, marking a process by which she herself begins to embody and to live them, so that she "becomes" their truth. Among the themes she develops are the quest for a *knowledge of one's soul,* the full *experience* of the present moment, *prayer* as a practice of clearing the pathway to the soul in which God resides and with whom the soul then communes, the cultivation of *solitude and silence* as forms of *detaching* from external stimuli and dependencies on others for the sake of finding the source of happiness within, *the single life* as an opportunity for sharing one's love with many as opposed to bestowing it largely on only one person and one's children, a *discipline* in one's work and concentration on the subject at hand, *simplicity* of speech and lifestyle, *humility* in acknowledging and admitting to one's weaknesses and confessing one's limited understanding of self and others, the *value of sadness and suffering* as a school of *patience* in the process of becoming aware, an *ethics of love* that governs one's relationship with self and others based on self-knowledge, a *surrender* to one's circumstances and an *acceptance of death* and the death of the ego, or false self, as a way of enlarging upon and enriching life, and the *cosmic unity of all things* in nature where things and creatures are all equally deserving of attention and love.

It is along these themes that the selections from her writings in this volume have been made. Cited in mostly chronological order, the selections are intended to highlight her thoughts on each theme and their gradual development. The themes are grouped under three headings: "The Self," including Etty's exploration of the soul, the self, or her interior landscape through prayer and the practices of solitude and silence; "The World," which she observes around her and her responses to it; and "Self and World as One" as she moves back and forth between the interior and exterior worlds and comes to see them as interconnected and one.

The Mysticism of Etty Hillesum

In order to assess the mystical nature of Etty's writings, it is necessary to first define mysticism in broad terms. Generally, mysticism describes a distinct way of seeing and approaching reality and the world around us. In the mystical way of seeing, ordinary life and everyday events are interpreted from the perspective of the extraordinary, the natural from the supernatural, the concrete from the position of the transcendent, the human from the view of the divine. Such a perspective becomes possible for those who surrender to the silent mystery of an incomprehensible God, relinquishing their own powers, allowing for an encounter with death and the possibility of a new birth, and falling into the so-called abyss of the unknown. Mystics are people who begin their quest for wisdom or for God not in the world of externals but in the microcosm of their own soul. There they allow themselves to be fully present to the experiences of a deep-felt joy or sorrow, of beauty or suffering, of gain or loss, so that these opposing poles might in time reconcile and grow and ripen into a harmonious whole. Once this inner harmony has grown from within and wells up as a peace that defies all rational explanation, mystics can carry this inner harmony *into* the world, thus becoming catalysts in the transformation *of* the world.

A distinctive mark of mystics is that to them the life of the spirit is more real than the life of the body, the interior more real than the exterior, the transcendent more true than what is matter-of-fact. From this vantage point resembling a bird's-eye view, they perceive the world, its creatures, and all that is

in it as being permeated by a divine unifying presence, bestowing on each creature and every thing the right to be treasured
and loved. Thus, mystics can detect the cosmic grandeur in the
smallest thing in nature, such as a pebble, a flower, a tree. They
can also discern the natural world as being permeated by the
spirit, so that moving back and forth between outer world and
inner world becomes almost effortless.

Mystical practices involve contemplation and a close listening to the inner voices of discord or harmony, a surveying of
the interior or submerged landscape of the soul and its foreign
and intrusive elements, prayer as an addressing of the Other,
or God, by which the soul and God are able to meet and mirror one another and unite, and a reflection on the newly gained
insights and vistas of one's interior life with the goal of apply-
ing these in shaping one's attitudes and perceptions. Mysticism
assumes that people have the capacity to experience God in
a direct, unmediated fashion. This capacity can be repressed
but not destroyed; it can be neglected but not eliminated. One
can nurture one's capacity of a God experience through the
practices and spiritual disciplines of prayer, contemplation, and
reflection. Moreover, one can draw on the writings of those
who have been generally considered mystics, those who have
given testimony to the depth and concreteness of their God
experience, those who have become masters in the art of perceiving reality increasingly more and more from the perspective
of the transcendent or the divine.

In Etty Hillesum's writings, the mystical characteristics nearly
leap off the page. One might even say that her journey into
the mystical way of life reads like a textbook case. This journey begins with her surrender into the unknown and the "new
birth" upon meeting Spier and becoming his patient. She had
to submit to his instructions and directions, relinquishing her
independence and efforts at control by allowing herself to be

guided into the uncharted territory of her soul. To Etty, the outside world representing war, the Nazi occupation, deprivations, and her own biological family offered little in terms of stability and peace. Since she could not change her outside world, she resolved to begin working on the world that lay within. Once she had embarked on the journey of paying attention to her soul and its interior workings by keeping a diary and listening to the voice within, she became aware of the intensity of her inner turmoil.

Nonetheless, she persisted in allowing herself to experience it all with a new-found awareness and a childlike curiosity, suffering from the fighting that occurred on the "small battlefield" of her soul, the extreme sensations of joy and sorrow, highs and lows, ecstasies and defeats. During this period, she also began noticing her shortcomings, an egocentricity, self-absorption, and possessiveness, a desire to receive and force love to come to her from outside, as well as a lack of humility and a streak of defiance. Once acknowledged, these intrusive elements in her soul's landscape seem to recede into the background, resulting in a gradually evolving inner harmony and peace. In the process, she is guided by the mystical practices that Spier himself seems to have observed: prayer and a posture of kneeling, contemplation and a courageous and unflinching listening to her inner voice, and reflection and meditation on the gained insights so as to adjust her attitudes toward others and her perceptions of the world.

Etty had resolved to nurture the experiences of God's presence within her by emulating her teacher, taking note of his counsel, and delving into the literature and books he was suggesting to her. Through the example of such mystics as the psalmists, the Apostle Paul, the apostles in the New Testament, St. John the Evangelist, St. Matthew, St. Augustine, St. Francis of Assisi, Meister Eckhart, Thomas à Kempis, and writers such as Fjodor Dostoevsky, C. G. Jung, Rainer Maria Rilke, and Oswald Chambers, she continued to be guided in how to go about viewing reality from the perspective of the divine. By such tutoring, she could conceive of all of creation as a unified whole, whose individual parts each had their right to be respected and loved. Etty makes frequent reference in her diaries to flowers in a vase and pine cones on her desk, the bleeding geranium in Spier's study, the cut twigs decorating the corner of a room, the flowering jasmine by her house, the lupines at Camp Westerbork, and the tree outside her window. In the beauty of the smallest pebble, the petals of a flower, the curling branches of a tree, she could detect the entire cosmos, and this discovery made her burst out with the exuberant pronouncement that life was beautiful and God was good. For the things of the natural world and its creatures were all reflecting God's splendor to her, so that even enemies and those whose hearts were filled with violence and rage were deserving of compassion and love. When Etty decided to volunteer working at the Nazi transit camp and insisted on remaining there against the urging of friends advising her to leave, it was from the conviction that she would be carrying her peace and love *into* the world in order to transform the world, at least to some small degree. In the end, moving back and forth between the two worlds of dreadful suffering and overflowing joy, between physical deprivation and the abundance of the interior life, became to her almost effortless. And it was then that her prior intimations were confirmed, namely, that an idea or the line of a Rilke poem was "more real...than moving a house" and life in the spirit more real than life in the body.

While Etty's body has never been found, her spirit lives on through her writings. It is this spirit that continues to teach and guide us today as we look for the meaning of life, for the soul of all things, for the eternal spirit that indwells our own, so that by yielding to her wisdom and mystical insights we might encounter the same God who once met Etty and to whom she so joyously and gladly responded by giving herself away in compassionate love for her fellow human beings and "as a balm for all wounds."

1

The Self

KNOWLEDGE OF THE SOUL

The soul of a person forms the stabilizing center and source of inner strength. Getting to know one's soul and obtaining a glimpse of its landscape can be painful. Etty receives a first "look" at her soul at a therapy session with Spier, or S., as she refers to him in her diaries. She finds that her soul is in chaos, and it frightens her to the point that she wishes herself dead. A lot of hard work would lie ahead for her to unearth this center and allowing it to come into full view, but she is up to the challenge. Gaining inklings of one's soul involves observing how one's perceptions and behavior have changed over time. How did one used to act, how does one act now, and at what point did one experience a sense of inner grounding, strength, health, well-being, and peace? Etty does precisely that. She recognizes that becoming familiar with her soul's landscape produces a sense of peace in her and compassion for others. By meditating and resting in herself, she experiences a self-forgetfulness that, in turn, allows for "God" and "Love" to enter her interior space. She calls this practice "spiritual hygiene." For Etty, the soul is the place where inner and outside worlds meet, two worlds of equal importance. As she discovers her center, this

25

terra incognita, *she senses a desire to help others discover theirs. But she recognizes the danger of overindulging in the exploration of the inner landscape and forgetting the purpose of this quest: being rid of the ego, of one's pretentiousness, of the false self in order to tackle work effectively and be of benefit to others. Coming to grips with life and resolving its complexities begins with getting to know one's center, acknowledging its presence, and giving it form and formulation. Thus, internal dissonances slowly begin to harmonize and one finds a basic tune or rhythm to live by.*

Dear Herr S.,[1]

I wrote you a whole long tale just now, but I think I'll spare you. Even now, reading it over, I can't help smiling. It's all so melodramatic and pompous. Sitting here peacefully at my familiar desk, with the blood coursing merrily through my veins thanks to your marvelous exercises, I feel like patting myself on the head in a motherly way and saying, "Now, now, my girl, everything'll be all right, just don't take yourself and your feelings and thoughts so seriously. You should really be rather ashamed of yourself."

You know, yesterday, when I could do nothing but look stupidly at you, I experienced such a clash of conflicting thoughts and feelings that I was quite shattered and would have yelled out loud had I had even less self-control. I experienced strong erotic feelings for you, which I thought I would have got over by now, and at the same time a strong aversion to you, and there was also a sudden feeling of utter loneliness, a suspicion that life is terribly difficult, that one has to face it all on one's own, that help from outside is out of the question, and uncertainty, fear, all of that, too. A small slice of chaos was suddenly staring at me from deep

---

1. This letter is the first entry in Exercise Book One; it probably was never sent to Julius Spier. Etty and Spier spoke only German together, hence the German address "Herr" (Mister).

down inside my soul. And when I had left you and was going back home, I wanted a car to run me over, and thought, ah, well, I must be out of my mind, like the rest of my family, something I always think when I feel the slightest bit desperate. But I know again now that I am not mad; I simply need to do a lot of work on myself before I develop into an adult and complete human being. And you will help me, won't you?

Well, I have written you a few lines now; they've cost me a lot of trouble. I write with the greatest reluctance, and always feel inhibited and uncertain when I do. Yet I want to become a writer one day, would you believe it?

Dear Herr S., until next time then, and thank you for all your kindness, and for all you have done for me already.

Etty Hillesum
— March 8, 1941, Saturday

Just now, when I was sitting on the dustbin in the sun out on our stony little terrace, with my head leaning against the wash-tub and with the sun on the strong, dark, still leafless branches of the chestnut tree, I had a very clear sense of the difference between then and now. And the things for which I needed a lot of words only this morning are now said quickly. The sun on the dark branches, the chirping birds, and me on the dust-bin in the sun. In the past I would sit like that quite often too, but except for just once I had never before felt as I did this afternoon. In the past, I took in the tree and the sun with my intellect. I wanted to put down so many words why I found it so beautiful, I wanted to understand how everything fitted together, I wanted to fathom that deep, that primitive feeling with my mind, or at least I think I did. In other words, I wanted to subject nature, everything, to myself, I felt obliged to inter-pret it. And the quite simple fact is that now I just let it happen to me. I go about filled with deep emotion, but it is no longer one that wears me out, rather one that gives me strength; health courses through my veins. As I sat there like that in the sun, I bowed my head unconsciously as if to take in even more of that new feeling for life. Suddenly I knew deep down how someone can sink impetuously to his knees and find peace there, his face hidden in his folded hands.

—March 16, 1941, Sunday, 4:30 p.m.

A human being is but a frail and fragile creature. But then, one cannot expect to feel elated all the time. And a little depression is not unhealthy either. As S. once put it: at the end of every day you ought to concentrate for ten minutes on how the day has gone, what good and what bad it has brought you, what unnecessary effort, etc....

"One ought to recognize the negative side of people in whose surroundings one lives, and guard against it, but that is no reason for rejecting and despising such people but rather for treating them with compassion."[2]

It seems so simple and almost trite, but if one really lived by this rule, allowed these few words to enter one's flesh and blood, then one would become a different human being.

Oh, S., how much I look forward to rushing back to your rooms tomorrow and how much I wonder what the afternoon will bring! Put like that, it seems a bit high-flown, and in fact I never really think about what the morrow will bring. In the past I used to indulge in the wildest fantasies and daydreams, which would then come slap up against a reality in which everything simply dwindled away, and the tears would come. All I know now is that I shall go to you tomorrow, and I accept everything in advance: if you are very businesslike, well and good, if you are very sweet, then that will be an unexpected bonus, will lend greater strength to my soul, oh dear, that's a bit too precious,

---

2. Quoting Spier's comments during the lectures he gave to students at his home.

but anyway, I don't imagine things in advance any longer and that is a fundamental difference from what used to happen.

"One cannot teach what one has not mastered oneself." You could well take that to heart, my girl!

"If someone can look further than others, thanks to more vigorous inner development, then this maturity must not be expressed in superiority over others who are less developed, but in tolerance, patience, and understanding."

All these quotations, which might, as it were, have been taken straight from my own heart, appeal to me so much because it is as if S. had been writing them for me personally. His expressive gray head, those eyes that light up now and then, are behind these words, and it is as if they were dictating these truths to me. In the past I would have nodded understandingly with an "Oh, how true," on reading them, but now they fill my entire being, sink to somewhere deep down in me and become part of myself.   — March 17, 1941, Monday, 10:30 p.m.

J.[3] "Once a person has a center, all external impressions can find an anchorage there (must call a halt there). Anyone who lacks a center and is uncertain, is thrown off balance by the least impression, grows increasingly uncertain, while the center of the former grows more constant with every impression."

---

3. The "J" refers to Carl Gustav Jung (1875–1961), a Swiss psychiatrist and the founder of analytical psychology, whom Etty is quoting here. The son of a Swiss Reformed pastor and former student and associate of Sigmund Freud, Jung had become convinced through the study of his patients and himself that life had a spiritual purpose beyond material goods and the outside world. A person's main task, he believed, was to discover and fulfill one's God-given, innate potential, much as the acorn contained the potential for becoming an oak tree. Based on his study of Christianity and other world religions, Jung concluded that the process of spiritual transformation is the mystical core of all religions. It is a process where one meets the self and at the same time the Divine. Unlike Sigmund Freud, Jung thought spiritual experience and discipline were essential to our well-being. Julius Spier had studied with Jung in Zurich and employed Jungian methods in his practice of psycho-chirology. Etty makes reference to several books by Jung, which she read in the original German, and his influence on Etty, both directly or indirectly through Spier, was immense.

My "center" is growing firmer by the day. In the past, for all my fine and well-founded theories, I was nothing but a fluttering, insecure little bird. And now, deep inside me, there is a center of strength which also radiates strength to the outside, as I can tell from the reactions of my fellow men.

And all this has nothing to do with being introverted. The strength comes from within, from a small, closed-in center, into which I sometimes withdraw completely if the outside world seems momentarily too rowdy for me, but for the rest, all my senses are focused on the outside reality, and what they observe there they convey to the center, which may thus be said to be reinforced by every new impression. Whereas in the past all outside impressions used to make me feel anxious and unsure. I would always have to choose then between two furiously alternating states: a state of total withdrawal from the outside world, of an inner harmony almost too beautiful to be true, so fragile and tender and so easily upset by the slightest jolt from the outside; and another state of being upset and consumed and thrown off balance and made uncertain by just about everything, if it were only reading a serial in a magazine or seeing the beautiful legs of a young girl walking past. My lack of such legs — even though mine will just about pass muster — would suddenly make me think that all my studies were a waste of time; not having perfect legs made me feel so depressed that all my pleasure in my work was gone, so much so that it would take a lot of energy to get me back to it. But now I must try to catch enough sleep, that's also part of healthy living. More tomorrow, good night!

—March 17, 1941, Monday, 10:30 p.m.

I think that I'll do it anyway: I'll "turn inward" for half an hour each morning before work, and listen to my inner voice. Lose myself. You could also call it meditation. I am still a bit weary of that word. But anyway, why not? A quiet half-hour within yourself. It's not enough just to move your arms and legs and all the other muscles about in the bathroom each morning. Man is body and spirit. And half an hour of exercises combined with half an hour of meditation can set the tone for the whole day.

But it's not that simple, that sort of "quiet hour." It has to be learned. A lot of unimportant inner litter and bits and pieces have to be swept out first. Even a small head can be piled high inside with irrelevant distractions. True, there may be edifying emotions and thoughts, too, but the clutter is ever present. So let this be the aim of the meditation: to turn one's innermost being into a vast empty plain, with none of that treacherous undergrowth to impede the view. So that something of "God" can enter you, and something of "Love," too. Not the kind of love-de-luxe that you revel in deliciously for half an hour, taking pride in how sublime you can feel, but the love you can apply to small, everyday things.

I might of course read the Bible each morning, but I don't think I'm ready for that. I still worry about the real meaning of the book, rather than lose myself in it.

I think I'll read a little bit of *In den Hof der Wijsbegeerte* (The mansion of philosophy) each morning instead. I might of course confine myself to writing a few words on these blue-lined pages. To the patient examination of just one single thought, even if none of my thoughts is very important. In the past, ambition stopped me from committing such trivia to paper. Everything had to be marvelous, perfect, I simply could not allow myself to write down any old thing, even though I was sometimes bursting with the longing to do just that.

And, for goodness' sake, stop looking at yourself in the mirror, Etty, you fool. It must be awful to be very beautiful, for then one would not bother to look farther inside, one would be so dazzled by the blinding exterior. Others, too, would respond to the beautiful exterior alone, so that one might actually shrivel up inside altogether.

The time I spend in front of the mirror, because I am suddenly caught by a funny or fascinating or interesting expression on this really not particularly pretty face of mine, could surely be spent on better things. It annoys me terribly, all this peering at myself....

I must learn to feel genuinely indifferent to my appearance, not to care in the least how I look. I must lead a much more inward life. With other people, too, I pay much too much attention to appearances, dwelling on their looks. Yet what really matters is man's soul or his essence or whatever else you care to call what shines through from within.

If you really want to turn your life into one great, unblemished and serious whole, my girl, then you are going to have to learn to forget a great many things and to tackle a lot of others more seriously. You are also going to have to organize your time better and not waste it on so many trifles. You are going to have to take honest stock of a mass of uncertainties still at large in your soul. You are going to have to go on taking stock of yourself. You are not going to be able to live a life free of supervision.

If you want to teach others how to live, you must first take yourself in hand. Above all, you must practice some spiritual "hygiene." Jung, I believe, calls it psychologically "housetrained." You are only a beginner, but at least you have made a beginning, and that is quite a lot to be going on with.

— June 8, 1941, Sunday morning, 9:30 a.m.

The landscape man carries within him he also seeks without. Perhaps that is why I have always had that strange longing for the wide Russian steppes. My inner landscape consists of great, wide plains, infinitely wide, with hardly a horizon in sight — one plain merging into the next. As I sit huddled up in this chair, my head bowed low, I roam across those bare plains, and when I have been sitting like that for a while, a feeling of well-being, of infinity and peace, comes over me.

The inner world is as real as the outer world. One ought to be conscious of that. It, too, has its landscape, contours, possibilities, its boundless regions. And man himself must be a small center in which the inner and outer worlds meet. These two worlds are fed by each other, you must not neglect one at the expense of the other, must not deem one more important than the other. Otherwise you impoverish your own personality. A great many people strike me as being divided in half and thus more or less disabled. That is probably because they have failed to recognize their inner world consciously as such. Now and then forces from the inner world make themselves felt and may to a certain extent widen people's horizons and give them an inkling of something of greater importance, but everything is too disorganized, too chaotic, barely conscious. Their inner world is fallow, uncultivated ground which does not seem worth tilling. It is *terra incognita*. And I sometimes feel the urge to start the work of reclamation, to create order and to bring it into consciousness. Who knows but in the long run that may be my life's work?

— June 11, 1941, Wednesday morning, 9:30 a.m.

Look here, my girl, all that is no doubt terribly important, that tremendously interesting spiritual life of yours and that interesting gentleman, but it is not what really matters, after all. What matters is to abandon that little ego of yours for work and for other people. I am once more most dissatisfied with you. You are again overindulging yourself with your soul. Once again you have lost yourself. Your depression has lifted, and you've taken enough time over it; another bit of order has been wrested from the chaos, but you have forgotten everything else. My belief is that you've been thinking yourself too important again. You must move on from the personal to the supra-personal, and

here you still have a lot to learn from him. Don't get bogged
down in petty details. Don't miss the forest for the trees....
   No one part should be the main thing in your life. The main
thing is the whole. Don't overemphasize any one thing; that way
your inner harmony will go haywire. You must remain detached
from everything you are interested in. You must not ally your
inner forces to any one thing, must not invest them in it, you
must keep your forces to yourself. And that's enough wisdom
for the moment.
   Once again, you must not want to possess another; make no
demands on him. That is something I have to relearn again and
again in my dealings with S.
                   — June 19, 1941, Thursday morning, 9:30 a.m.

There is nothing else for it, I shall have to solve my own problems. I always get the feeling that when I solve them for myself
I shall have also solved them for a thousand other women. For
that very reason I must come to grips with myself. But life is
certainly very difficult, particularly if you can't find the words.
   All this devouring of books from early youth has been nothing but laziness on my part. I allow others to formulate what
I ought to be formulating myself. I keep seeking outside confirmation of what is hidden deep inside me, when I know that
I can reach clarity only by using my own words. I really must
abandon that laziness, and particularly my inhibitions and inse-
curity, if I am ever to find myself, and through myself, find
others. I must have clarity, and I must learn to accept myself.
And now I must go to the market and buy a melon. Everything
feels so heavy inside me, and I want so much to feel light.
   For years I have bottled everything up; it all goes into some
great reservoir, but it will all have to come out again, or I shall
know that I have lived in vain, that I have taken from mankind
and given nothing back. I sometimes feel I am a parasite, and
that depresses me and makes me wonder if I lead any kind

of useful life. Perhaps my purpose in life is to come to grips with myself, properly to grips with myself, with everything that bothers and tortures me and clamors for inner solution and formulation. For these problems are not just mine alone. And if at the end of a long life I am able to give some form to the chaos inside me, I may well have fulfilled my own small purpose. Even while I write this down, my unconscious is protesting at such expressions as "purpose" and "mankind" and "solutions of problems." I find them pretentious. But then I'm such an ingenuous and dull young woman, still so lacking in courage.

No, my friend, you are not there yet by a long way; you ought really to be kept away from all the great philosophers until you have learned to take yourself a little more seriously. I think I'd better buy that melon first, and take it to Nethes[4] tonight. That's also part of living, isn't it?

I feel just like a dustbin sometimes, what with all the murkiness, conceitedness, halfheartedness, and second-rateness inside me! But there's also a genuine uprightness and an almost elementary passion for imposing some cleanliness and for discovering the harmony between without and within.

Sometimes I long for a convent cell, with the sublime wisdom of centuries set out on bookshelves all along the wall and a view across the cornfields — there must be cornfields and they must wave in the breeze — and there I would immerse myself in the wisdom of the ages and in myself. Then I might perhaps find peace and clarity. But that would be no great feat. It is right here, in this very place, in the here and now, that I must find them. I must fling myself into reality, time and again, must come to terms with everything I meet on my path, feed the outer world with my inner world and vice versa. But it is all so terribly difficult, and I feel so heavyhearted. . . .

---

4. The family from which Spier rented rooms.

All the melons will probably be gone by now. I feel as if I were moldering inside, as if I were plugged up, and my body hurts. But don't delude yourself, Etty, it's not really your body, it's your ravaged little soul that afflicts you.

In a little while I shall no doubt be writing how beautiful life really is and how happy I am, but at the moment I can't even imagine what that feels like.

I still lack a basic tune; a steady undercurrent; the inner source that feeds me keeps drying up, and worse still, I think much too much. My ideas hang on me like outsize clothes into which I still have to grow. My mind lags behind my intuition. This is not altogether a bad thing. But it means that my mind or my reason, or whatever you care to call it, must sometimes work overtime in order to seize the various premonitions by their coattails. A host of vague ideas keeps clamoring for concrete formulation. I must stop and listen to myself, sound my own depths, eat well, and sleep properly if I am to keep my balance, or it will turn into something altogether too Dostoevskian. But alas the emphasis these days is on speed, not on rest.   — August 4, 1941, Monday, 2:30 p.m.

I still can't write. I want to write about the reality behind things, and that's beyond my ken still. The only thing I'm really concerned with is the atmosphere, you might say the "soul," and so the substance goes on eluding me. As a result I lack a firm foothold. You have to describe the concrete, the down-to-earth reality, and so illume it with your words, with your spirit, that the soul behind it is evoked. If you allude directly to the so-called soul, then everything becomes too vague, too formless. If I really get it into my head more and more firmly that I want to write, do nothing but write, then I must also realize that I am preparing a cross for my back — I already feel it every now and then and shudder a little. The question is whether I have the talent for it.

Yet I must start slowly on that great block of uncut granite I carry within me if I am to model my small figures, or else I am bound to get crushed one day. If I don't seek and discover my form, I will end up in night and in chaos, something of which I keep getting strong intimations even now.

— August 5, 1941, Tuesday, 12 noon

EXPERIENCING IT ALL

Getting acquainted with one's soul involves both mind and heart. The mind and the intellect formulate and process ideas, while the heart allows for feeling them and becoming vulnerable to them. Knowledge of the soul's landscape and its dynamics has a personal dimension, namely, observing the feelings accompanying what one sees within and without, and the courage to be oneself. Etty is passionate about bringing the tools of intellect and feeling into harmony within her. But first she will need to discipline herself to live in the here and now, rather than reveling in an illusionary future or being afraid of it. She will need to experience the present moment, become passive in receiving the present without escaping from it. In order to do so, she clings to the phrase "living with one's pauses." Etty had heard the phrase from Spier: living in the here and now and concentrating on the present moment while allowing for periods of inner rest. The last sentence in Exercise Book Eleven is written in all caps and reads, "One must acknowledge one's pauses!" For it is during such pauses that spirit and mind, feeling and thinking, the inside and the outside worlds can be received, perceived, and given time to reconcile in the soul into a dynamic and peaceful harmony.

This vague fear is something else I must conquer in myself. Life is difficult, it is true, a struggle from minute to minute (don't overdo it now, Etty!), but the struggle itself is thrilling. In the past I would live chaotically in the future, because I refused to live in the here and now. I wanted to be handed everything on a platter, like a badly spoiled child. Sometimes I had the certain if rather undefined feeling that I would "make it" one day, that I had the capacity to do something "extraordinary," and at other times the wild fear that I would "go to the dogs" after all. I now realize why. I simply refused to do what needed to be done, what lay right under my nose. I refused to climb into the future one step at a time. And now, now that every minute is so full, so chock-full of life and experience and struggle and victory and defeat, and more struggle and sometimes peace, now I no longer think of the future, that is, I no longer care whether or not I shall "make it," because I now have the inner certainty that everything will be taken care of. Before, I always lived in anticipation, I had the feeling that nothing I did was the "real" thing, that it was all a preparation for something else, something "greater," more "genuine." But that feeling has dropped away from me completely. I live here and now, this minute, this day, to the full, and life is worth living. And if I knew that I was going to die tomorrow, then I would say: it's a great shame, but it's been good while it lasted. I put that forward, in theory, before, one summer evening — I still remember it well — with Frans on the Reijnders' little terrace. But what I felt then was resignation, not acceptance, something like, well if it's all up with me tomorrow, I shan't bother my head too much. That's life for you. And we know life, don't we? We have experienced everything, if only in the mind, and there's no need any longer to hang on for dear life. Something like that, I believe. We were very old then, very wise, and very weary. But now it is quite different. And so to work.

— March 21, 1941, Friday, 8:30 a.m.

I am not yet sufficiently at one with life; I am not firmly rooted in it. That is no doubt because my physical and spiritual sides have not yet fused into a single, organic whole. From time to time the meaning of everything suddenly escapes me. That is probably due to a lack of self-confidence, to a lack of faith in myself, to not believing that what one does is good and meaningful. And if one does not see any meaning in one's own life, then the whole of life is suddenly without meaning as well. Oh, Etty, you're a strange case. I shall probably never go mad, at least I no longer think so, but I can well understand why people do. I still want to lose myself in everyone and in everything — a feeling of wanting to live in harmony with all that exists. I haven't yet learned to accept life's many contradictions with the core of my being rather than with my intellect. What I want is total harmony and unity and peace. I would like to disappear, to dissolve, to forget and be rid of myself. Not running away from myself, but merging quite naturally and harmoniously with the earth and the sky. I really don't yet know what is and what is not important. Where the center of gravity of my life should be. Or whether what I am doing is useful. I am not committed to anything. I don't live by people's usual standards, I have no steady job, I am not married, and I still lack the courage to declare, "I like the way I live, I don't need outside standards to live by, my standards are to be found in my innermost being." Whenever I start brooding the way I am doing now, I can feel the headache and the nausea mounting on all sides.   — Deventer,[5] August 7, 1941, Thursday

Referring to a letter written to Spier while at her family's home in Deventer:

Here in this strange family, there is such an indescribable mixture of barbarism and culture that you are stripped of all your strength. My older brother is always saying, "What we have

---

5. Etty's parents lived in Deventer, about two hours by train east of Amsterdam; she was visiting them and staying at their house for about a week.

here is organized disorder." So much capital lies scattered about here, so much capital of spiritual and human values, but all it does is lie about, badly managed and without any purpose. Sometimes one feels so sad and heavy-hearted because of it all. In the past my picturesque family would cost me a bucket of desperate tears every night. I can't explain those tears as yet; they came from somewhere in the dark collective unconscious. Nowadays I am not so wasteful of this precious fluid, but all the same it is not easy to live here.

But I did not really set out to write about this complicated household. What I wanted to write about was your letter, which brought some order into this chaos and was tremendously important to me. When that kindly, dependable, much longed-for handwriting looked out at me from the letterbox, I was overjoyed. Then I read your letter, but at first I felt quite out of touch with it. And also out of touch with you. I stood there completely cut off and alienated as I had stood a thousand times earlier in my life. A lack of continuity, my greatest inner danger.

Later I flung myself onto my bed, once again deciphered your hieroglyphics and suddenly everything was back in place. I regained contact with myself, with the deepest and best in me, which I call God, and so also with you. A moment came in which I grew one stage further, in which many new perceptions about myself and my bond with you and my fellow beings appeared. A few days have gone by since then, and that moment, so important to me, lies within me like a rounded and complete whole, but still I cannot find the words to set it all down.

Do you know that when it comes to "being true to themselves," most people are real amateurs? I, too. And if one lacks the courage to be oneself, then one also has no courage for others. One has no contact with one's fellow beings, feels lonely, and around that loneliness one spins all sorts of interesting theories, for instance the one about the "misunderstood soul," etc., but all that is nothing but false romanticism and a built-in escape. And because you are someone who has the courage to live life to the full, which simply means living on one's own original sources, you force any who grapple with you seriously to return to their sources, to themselves and thence to others. And I am so grateful for having been allowed to come so close to you; that will be of crucial importance in my further development — I feel that more and more strongly. You are, in fact the first person to whom I have ever related inwardly, whom I have tried to emulate. Perhaps it will be the first "non-amateurish" friendship of my whole life. If, thanks to you, I take seriously the problems that come my way, and if I deal with them — well, a great many things in my life will then have been clarified.

— August 10, 1941, Sunday morning, in bed, the only place in this house where one can be alone

I am getting on famously, truly. I am pulling through. If things go on as they are I shall have a jar full of white pebbles.[6] But right now I am dead tired. A strong straight pillar is growing in my heart. I can almost feel it growing, and around it all the rest revolves: I myself, the world, everything. And the pillar is an earnest of my inner security. How terribly important this is for me, being in touch with my inner self! I don't go on losing my balance or tumbling from one world into the next, and I no longer view the physical world with such amazement from the perspective of the intellectual world, and vice versa. Something is being consolidated within me, I seem to be taking root instead of continuously drifting, but it is still no more than the fragile start of a new and more mature phase. You must keep watching your step, little one, but I am well pleased with you all the same;

---

6. Etty had read about the practice of evaluating the day in the evening: putting a white pebble in a jar meant the day had been good, a black pebble that it had been bad.

you're pulling through, truly, you are pulling through. And now I'm going to go and collapse in bed, tomorrow is another day to be lived to the full.   —August 10, 1941, Sunday, midnight

Life is composed of tales waiting to be retold by me. Oh, what nonsense — I don't really know anything. I am unhappy again. I can quite see why people get drunk or go to bed with a total stranger. But that isn't really my way. I must keep sober, keep a clear head. And do it alone. It is just as well that that villain wasn't in tonight. Otherwise I should have run to him again saying, "Please help me, I am so unhappy, I am bursting apart at the seams." And I expect others to straighten things out for themselves! "Listen to your inner voice." Yes, indeed. So I withdrew to the farthest corner of my little room, sat on the floor, squeezed myself in between two walls, my head bowed. Yes. And sat there. Absolutely still, contemplating my navel so to speak, in the pious hope that new sources of inspiration would bubble up inside me. My heart was once again frozen and would not melt; every outlet was blocked and my brain squeezed by a large vice. And what I am waiting for whenever I sit huddled up like that is for something to give, for something to start flowing inside me.

I really took on too heavy a burden when I read all those letters from his girlfriend. I had always warded her off in ostrich-like fashion, and now she's caught up with me all the same. Those letters raise a whole lot of problems, but I keep struggling along. I wish I were completely uncomplicated, like that man tonight, or like a field of grass. I still take myself too seriously. On days like this I am sure that no one suffers as much as I do. Imagine somebody in pain all over his body, unable to bear anyone touching him even with the tip of a finger — that's the feeling in my soul, or whatever you want to call it. The smallest pressure causes pain. A soul without a skin, as

Annie Romein[7] once wrote about Carry van Bruggen. I would like to travel to faraway places. And see other people, who need have no names. Sometimes I feel as if the people with whom I have really close contact rob me of my vision. My vision of what? Etty, you really are being a bit devious and not very conscientious. You should be able to trace the real reason for your melancholy and for your awful headache. But alas, you're not really interested in doing so. You are just plain lazy. Lord, grant me a little humility.

Am I too busy? I want to know this century of ours inside and out. I feel it every day anew. I run my fingertips along the contours of these times. Or is that pure fiction?

But I always project myself back into reality. I make myself confront everything that crosses my path, which sometimes leaves me feeling battered. It is just as if I let myself crash violently into myself; leaving dents and scratches. But I imagine that it has to be like that. I sometimes feel I am in some blazing purgatory and that I am being forged into something else. But into what? I can only be passive, allow it to happen to me. But then I also have the feeling that all the problems of our age and of mankind in general have to be battled out inside my little head. And that means being active. Well, the worst of it is now past. I tore round the Skating Club like a drunken fool and addressed a few stupid remarks to the moon. The moon, too, wasn't born yesterday. No doubt he has looked down on plenty of characters like me, seen a thing or two. Well, well. A hard life is in store for me. Sometimes I don't feel like carrying on. At the moments when I feel I know exactly what is going to happen to me, what life will be like, I get so tired and feel no

---

7. A. H. M. Romein-Verschoor (1895–1978) was a Dutch historian, who had written a literary and sociological study of Dutch women novelists published in 1936. Etty refers to Romein's description of Caroline Lea van Bruggen-de Haan (1881–1932), a Dutch Jewish novelist famous for her psychological novels and somewhat critical of contemporary Jewish life in the Netherlands.

need to experience things as they come. But life always gains the upper hand, and then I find everything "interesting" and exciting again, and I am full of courage and full of ideas. One "must acknowledge one's pauses," but I wilt during the "pauses," or so it seems to me. And now goodnight.
— September 4, 1941, Tuesday night, 10:30 p.m.

The block started on Friday — that's when my organizing powers went out of the window. In the morning I had an experience and thought that's something I shall have to write about tonight. And I patted myself on the back with "Right then, tonight I shall 'go to work on myself.' " But then that damned Aleida[8] had to put her oar in. Her voice still shrills in my ear when I think of it. My God, what a person. She translates Dostoevsky,[9] and there is a Madonna in her room which she illuminates with concealed lighting when visitors turn up. But she thinks all eighty million Germans must be exterminated. Not a single one must be left alive. This because I said in all innocence that I could not live with the kind of hatred so many people nowadays force upon themselves against their better nature. And then it all came bursting out. How ugly, how degrading, how horrible! Oh, well, perhaps I'm lacking in patriotic fervor. Thinking back on the

---

8. Aleida Gerarda Schot (1900–1969) was a classmate of Etty's in Russian class and had been active as a freelance Russian translator since 1936; she published numerous Russian translations and was well respected for her work.

9. Fyodor Dostoevsky (1821–1881) was a Russian novelist, whose literary work explored from a psychological perspective the human condition in the troubled social and political context of nineteenth-century Russia. Dostoevsky was arrested and imprisoned in 1849 for his liberal views. His experiences in a prison camp in Siberia resulted in major changes in his political and religious convictions: he became disillusioned with Western ideas and philosophical movements, such as nihilism or socialism, paying greater tribute to traditional, rural-based rustic Russian values; and he underwent a religious conversion, which greatly strengthened his Christian, and specifically Orthodox, faith. Among his major works are *Crime and Punishment, Memoirs from the House of the Dead, The Idiot,* and *The Brothers Karamazov;* all of these Etty mentions as well as making a reference to Dostoevsky's four-year stay at the Siberian labor camp "with the Bible as his only reading matter."

conversation, I get the feeling that what I was dealing with was someone abnormal. But it was interesting, too. "Oh, I just gloat," she said, "when I stand by my window at night and hear the planes overhead." And it was as if her bosom were heaving and her nostrils flaring, although she has no bosom to speak of and a silly little nose.

Then I went home, thinking, "I simply must get down to some writing," and ended up with Bernard[10] and Parijs instead. I burst into the room with, "Tell me, do you also think that every last German ought to be exterminated?" "Yes, of course," came the answer. And a furious and passionate discussion ensued. One could write a whole pamphlet on that one evening.

To bed at half past twelve. And no "working on myself." That's where I believe things started to go wrong. But an evening of argument like that does get my blood up. . . . But one thing is certain: I must not keep getting tired. I *must* be prepared and vigilant. It's not *what* you experience but *how* you experience it that matters. When you feel dull and tired, the whole world becomes dull and tired. I don't believe in objective values. . . .   — September 29, 1941, Monday, 9:30 p.m.

This morning I stood in the bathroom waving my arms about, stark naked as usual, when I suddenly stopped and said very decidedly to my own mirror image, "Yes, I do have ideas of my own."

But I mustn't have too many ideas. When I was an innocent babe in arms I once wrote on a scrap of paper, "My ideas hang about me like clothes that are much too big and into which I still have to grow."

---

10. Bernard Meijlink was one of the boarders at Han Wegerif's, and he had suggested to Etty that she see Spier, whom he knew through his fiancée's sister, Gera Bongers, a student of Spier's.

And now the clothes are still too big. I can't grow quickly enough to fit them. I still revel too much in ideas, and I still lack the courage and self-confidence to give them concrete form.
— October 2, 1941, Thursday morning, 8:00 a.m.

I have a primitive longing to be simple, to live for the day, to "roll melodiously out of God's hand."

But pay attention now as you try to put it all into words. Emotion and reason, soul and mind may have been at loggerheads again, obscuring and weakening each other. Best to live in your emotions as smoothly and harmoniously and happily and dreamily as you like while your mind gets on with work in its own sphere. Spirit and mind should feed each other, should not be allowed to weaken each other. What you must not do is rely on some external certainty, and that means being secure in yourself and at peace with yourself, but also that your mind is allowed to explore restlessly and passionately what makes life hang together, not because you want to achieve something or want to succeed at something that interests you, but because you happen to have been created with a passionate and honest concern for what goes on in this world, and above all for what goes on in your inner world.

You shouldn't live on your brains alone but on deeper, more abiding sources, though you should gratefully accept your brains as a precious tool for delving into what problems your soul brings forth. To put it more soberly, what all of this means for me is probably that I should have greater trust in my intuition.

In fact it also means believing in God, without weakening; if anything, it gives you greater strength.

DEVELOPMENT DOES NOT TAKE TIME INTO ACCOUNT.
— October 7, 1941, Tuesday morning, 9:00 a.m.

Something else: I have learned one important thing today: wherever you happen to find yourself, be there with your whole heart. If your heart is elsewhere, you won't give enough to the community in which you happen to be, and that community will be the poorer for it. Whether it's office girls on the make, or God knows what, you must belong to it wholeheartedly, and you must just discover that there's something to them as well.

— July 27, 1942, Monday, after 10:30 p.m.

PRAYER AS PATHWAY TO THE SOUL

Addressing and communicating with God in prayer can take the form of adoration, petition, confession, intercession, and praise. Prayer can be spoken or silent, verbalized or interiorized, and can be accompanied by such postures as kneeling, folding one's hands, bowing one's head. All these forms and postures are recorded in Etty's writings. To begin with, her prayer springs from a desire to come to know her soul and to bring order to her interior chaos. The practice is encouraged by Spier, who himself prayed daily and whom she sought to emulate. At first she mentions God's name mostly in colloquial expressions, such as "God knows"; then the name is used as a personal address alternating between "God" and "Lord." The prayers in her diaries are initially brief, some consisting of only a sentence or two. They lengthen with Spier's death, her arrival at Wester-bork, and the dissolution of the Jewish Council, hence when her own and her family's deportation become almost certain. The "girl who could not kneel" gradually became the one who could do so quite easily and, in time, could pray without ceasing at virtually any moment without the need for privacy or a certain posture. Initially drawn to the practice of daily prayer for its calming effects and the sense of serenity it produced, Etty later is in a type of ongoing conversation and dialogue with God; her attitude toward life and work are shaped by continuous prayer.

I am full of unease, a strange, infernal agitation, which might be productive if only I knew what to do with it. A "creative" unease. Not of the body — not even a dozen passionate nights of love could assuage it. It is almost a "sacred" unease. "Oh God, take me into Your great hands and turn me into Your instrument, let me write...."

In Deventer the days were like great sunny plains, each one a long, uninterrupted whole; there was contact with God and with every person I met, possibly because I met so few. There were cornfields I shall never forget, whose beauty nearly brought me to my knees; there were the banks of the Ijssel with the colorful parasols and the thatched roofs and the patient horses. And the sun, which I drank in through all my pores.

And back here each day are a thousand fragments, the great plain is no more, and God, too, has departed. If this continues much longer, then I'm bound to start asking myself about the meaning of life all over again, and that never means plumbing philosophical depths but is proof positive that things are going badly with me.   — July 4, 1941, Friday

There is a really deep well inside me. And in it dwells God. Sometimes I am there, too. But more often stones and grit block the well, and God is buried underneath. Then He must be dug out again.

I imagine that there are people who pray with their eyes turned heavenward. They seek God outside themselves. And there are those who bow their head and bury it in their hands. I think that these seek God inside.

                              — August 26, 1941, Tuesday evening

I make very high demands on myself and in inspired moments consider myself quite capable of meeting them, but inspiration doesn't last forever, and in my more mundane moods I am filled with sudden fears that I might not fulfill the promise of those "exalted" moments. But why do I have to achieve things? All I need do is to "be," to live and to try being a little bit human. One can't control everything with the brain; must allow one's emotions and intuitions free play as well. Knowledge is power, and that's probably why I accumulate knowledge, out of a desire to be important. I don't really know. But Lord, give me wisdom, not knowledge. Or rather the knowledge that leads to wisdom and true happiness and not the kind that leads to power. A little peace, a lot of kindness, and a little wisdom — whenever I have these inside me I feel I am doing well.

—September 5, 1941, Friday morning, 9:00 a.m.

There is a sort of lamentation and loving-kindness as well as a little wisdom somewhere inside me that cry to be let out. Sometimes several different dialogues run through me at the same time, images and figures, moods, a sudden flash of something that must be my very own truth. Love for human beings that must be hard fought for. Not through politics or a party, but in myself. Still a lot of false shame to get rid of. And there is God. The girl who could not kneel but learned to do so on the rough coconut matting in an untidy bathroom. Such things are often more intimate than sex. The story of the girl who gradually learned to kneel is something I would love to write in the fullest possible way.

—November 22, 1941, Saturday morning

The first longer prayer in her diaries recorded after a brief prayer early in the evening the prior day, which Etty had closed by saying, "All of a sudden I am in a very strange mood."

Something has happened to me, and I don't know if it's just a passing mood or something crucial. It is as if I had been pulled back abruptly to my roots and had become a little more self-reliant and independent.

Last night, cycling through cold, dark Lairessestraat — if only I could repeat everything I babbled out then! Something like this: "God, take me by your hand, I shall follow You dutifully and not resist too much. I shall evade none of the tempests life has in store for me, I shall try to face it all as best I can. But now and then grant me a short respite. I shall never again assume, in my innocence, that any peace that comes my way will be eternal. I shall accept all the inevitable tumult and struggle. I delight in warmth and security, but I shall not rebel if I have to suffer cold, should You so decree. I shall follow wherever Your hand leads me and shall try not to be afraid. I shall try to spread some of my warmth, of my genuine love for others, wherever I go. But we shouldn't boast of our love for others. We cannot be sure that it really exists. I don't want to be anything special, I only want to be true to that in me which seeks to fulfill its promise. I sometimes imagine that I long for the seclusion of a nunnery. But I know that I must seek You among people, out in the world." And that is what I shall do, despite the weariness and dislike that sometimes overcomes me. I vow to live my life out there to the full. Sometimes I think that my life is only just beginning. That the real difficulties are still to come, although at times I feel that I have struggled through so many already. I shall study and try to comprehend, I shall allow myself to become thoroughly perplexed by whatever comes my way and apparently diverts me, yes, I shall allow myself to be perplexed time and again perhaps, in order to arrive at greater certainty. Until I am no longer perplexed and a state of balance has been achieved, but with all paths still open to me.

—November 25, 1941, Tuesday morning, 9:30 a.m.

I kneel once more on the rough coconut matting, my hands over my eyes and pray: "Oh, Lord, let me feel at one with myself. Let me perform a thousand daily tasks with love, but let every one spring from a greater central core of devotion and love." Then it won't really matter what I do and where I am. But I still have a long way to go.

I shall swallow twenty quinine pills today; I feel a bit peculiar down there, south of my midriff.

— December 3, 1941, Wednesday morning, 8:00 a.m.
in the bathroom

Dear Lord, I can't call upon you on every silly occasion. That one time[11] when I called upon you with honest passion, out of a deep need, still gives me strength and has had a lasting effect.

The dark branches are swishing past my dim window. I shall go and put on my black dress now and paint my lips red; then the blind Hungarian and my deaf friend will turn up and lots of other people, and I'll just have to see again what life brings. If you just make up your mind to enter into every moment of this life and don't resist or cut yourself off, if you realize that it doesn't matter where you are and what you do, if you just have God in you — up you get, this instant.

— December 11, 1941, Thursday, 4:30 p.m.

Last night, shortly before going to bed, I suddenly went down on my knees in the middle of this large room, between the steel chairs and the matting. Almost automatically. Forced to the ground by something stronger than myself. Some time ago I said to myself, "I am a kneeler in training." I was still embarrassed by this act, as intimate as gestures of love that cannot be put into words either, except by a poet.

A patient once said to S., "I sometimes have the feeling that God is right inside me, for instance when I hear the *St. Matthew Passion*."[12] And S. said something like, "At such moments you

---

11. Her impetuous request of God for a sign to receive clarity about her vocation and calling on November 24, 1941, leading to her first longer prayer, recorded above; for the request she made, see "On the discipline of work."

12. Presumably the St. Matthew Passion by Johann Sebastian Bach.

are completely at one with the creative and cosmic forces that are at work in every human being." And these creative forces are ultimately part of God, but you need courage to put that into words.

This phrase has been ringing in my ears for several weeks: you need courage to put that into words. The courage to speak God's name. S. once said to me that it took quite a long time before he dared to say "God" without feeling that there was something ridiculous about it. Even though he was a believer. And he said he prayed every night, prayed for others. And, shameless and brazen as always, wanting to know everything there is to know, I asked, "What exactly do you say when you pray?" And he was suddenly overcome with embarrassment, this man who always has clear, glass-bright answers to all my most searching and intimidating questions, and he said shyly: "That I cannot tell you. Not yet. Later."

— December 13, 1941, Sunday, 10:30 a.m.

After several days of reading Rainer Maria Rilke's The Book of Hours:[13]

Great confidence, truly great confidence, has very slowly been maturing in me of late. Feeling safe and secure in Your hands, oh God. I am no longer cut off quite so often from that deep undercurrent within me. And when I feel fervent and elated, then it is neither forced nor wayward but based on the certainty of that undercurrent. Nor do I still keep bumping into the sharp corners of the day.

— December 21, 1941, Sunday morning, 9:30 a.m.

---

13. Rainer Maria Rilke (1875–1926) was born in the city of Prague, which at that time was part of Austria. After his university studies he traveled widely in Italy and Russia and embarked on a literary career, developing a new style of poetry, marked by the visual arts. At the time of his death from leukemia, his work was greatly admired by many leading European artists, intellectuals, and writers. Rilke also was an avid letter writer and hundreds of letters and private correspondence make up the larger portion of his work, in addition to poetry, novels, and plays. Etty quotes Rilke throughout her diaries, especially from his collected *Letters* and *The Book of Hours.*

And now it is almost 8:30 p.m. The last evening of a year that has been my richest and most fruitful and, yes, the happiest of all. And if I had to put in a nutshell what this year has meant — from February 3, when I shyly pulled the bell at 27 Courbetstraat and a weird-looking character wearing some sort of antenna on his head examined my palms — then I would say: greater awareness and hence easier access to my inner sources. In the past I, too, used to be one of those who occasionally exclaimed, "I *really* am religious, you know." Or something like that. But now I sometimes actually drop to my knees beside my bed, even on a cold winter night. And I listen in to myself; allow myself to be led, not by anything on the outside, but by what wells up from deep within. It's still no more than a beginning, I know. But it is no longer a shaky beginning, it has already taken root.   —December 31, 1941, Wednesday, 8:30 p.m.

That is really the worst that can happen: as if your inner light switch had been turned off, or, let us put it boldly, as if God had deserted you for a moment. But last night, driven by [an] unexpected welling up of inner plentitude, I had to kneel down again suddenly in the middle of the room, and when I woke up the gray dawn was no longer a piece of paper but had the spacious dimensions of old.
          —January 4, 1942, Monday morning, 9:30 a.m.

God, I thank You for having given me so much strength: the inner center regulating my life is becoming stronger and more pivotal all the time.

My many conflicting outside impressions now get on wonderfully well with one another. My inner space is able to encompass more and more, and the many conflicts no longer deprive one another of life nor do they stand in one another's way, and after a day like yesterday I feel entitled to say with some conviction: peace reigns in my inner domain because a powerful central authority is in control there.

I think I work well with You, God, that we work well together. I have assigned an ever larger dwelling space to You, and I am also beginning to become faithful to You. I hardly ever have to deny You any more. Nor, at frivolous and shallow moments, do I have to deny my own inner life any longer out of a sense of shame. The powerful center spreads its rays to the outermost boundaries. I am no longer ashamed of my deeper moments, I no longer pretend from time to time not to recognize them.

Yesterday morning: at my desk, immersed in the undercurrent, and in the evening the theatrical atmosphere at the Levies.[14] At the Levies I defended Tideman[15] against all their criticism. There is no conflict in me any longer. Rilke and Marlene Dietrich[16] tolerate each other, as it were, wonderfully well in me. I don't have to deny either for a single moment in order to appreciate the other to the full. What a silly comparison really, how did that occur to me? And that intense conversation with Jan Polak. It was only thanks to that that I realized I can put into words what touches me, have the courage to say what I feel. Almost to bear witness to it. A great deal happened yesterday; it was a rich day, full to overflowing again, too much to be written up in full. And now to work.

I thank You, God, peace and quiet now reign in my great inner Domain, thanks to the strong central authority You exert.

---

14. Referring to the residence of Werner and Liesl Levie.

15. Henny "Tide" Tideman was part of the Spier circle and Etty's best friend. Tide was a devout Christian and a member of the Oxford Club. One aspect of her faith practice was to have daily moments of silence when she intently listened to God; the thoughts that came to her during that time she considered divinely inspired. It is possible that the latter practice of hers was the subject of the Levies' criticism.

16. Marlene Dietrich (1901–92) was a German-born actress, singer, and prominent frontline entertainer to the Allied troops during World War II. Etty would have heard her singing on the radio.

The furthest flung boundaries sense Your authority and Your love and allow themselves to be guided by You.

> —January 9, 1942, Friday morning, 9:30 a.m.

God, I thank You. I thank You for wanting to dwell within me. I thank You for everything.

> —January 15, 1942, Thursday, 8:00 a.m.

The pink flowering cherry against the gray curtain is slowly beginning to die. The purple tulips are still twining whimsically and proudly into the air, but several are now falling sadly apart. Käthe's[17] drainpipe is frozen, women are walking about in trousers and men with scarves round their heads, we get green peas and potato flower in our bread, my little cyclist is so hungry and in Russia it is even colder. Tonight it felt so nice and cozy to be back in my lonely narrow bed. I thanked God again, not for the warm bed and the pea soup but for wanting to dwell in me once more. I never thank Him for the worldly goods He gives me, nor should I rebel against Him were he to cut them off. It goes against the grain to give thanks for something so many people lack. Things are not what they should be with the distribution of worldly goods on this imperfect earth of ours. And it seems to me a matter of pure chance whether one ends up among the sated or the hungry. I shall never be able to give thanks for my daily bread when I know that so many others do not have theirs. But I hope I shall be thankful for something else. For having God dwell in me. And that has nothing to do with being well fed. At least that is what I tell myself now, by my warm stove and after a decent breakfast. Truly, things are not nearly as simple as they seem.

> —January 23, 1942, Friday morning, 8:00 a.m.

---

17. Käthe Fransen was the live-in German cook employed by Wegerif; to Etty, she was like a substitute mother.

This morning I suddenly found myself kneeling beside the cold stove in the living room, saying, "Dear God, give me a little patience and a little love for the small things in my daily life. Don't let me be irritated by Han's[18] interminable coughing." I sometimes suspect him of coughing harder than necessary for purely dramatic effect. But I must remember that the need to dramatize is part of his illness and that he probably suffers more from that melodramatic state than from the illness itself. . . .

And later, "And let me also have a little more compassion and understanding for Bernard's ever-hungry stomach and not always think he's being greedy, and sincerely stop begrudging him every bite."

The boy is actually going hungry, and I have no fellow feeling for him at all because I look on him as a materialist with nothing on his mind but eating. But I must try to remember that this boy works terribly hard, rides long distances through the cold to get to his work, has lost a lot of weight, and is always hungry. My attitude to him is actually not far from being inhuman. — And so on.

— February 21, 1942, Saturday morning, 9:30 a.m.

Last night at 10:30 when I came back to my little room, where the curtains at the one large window are always left open, there it stood, my poor, ravaged lonely tree. A hesitant star climbed up its austere body, rested for a moment in the crook of one of its limbs (?!good!) and then lost itself in the wide sky, no longer caught up in the branches. The Rijksmuseum looked like a turreted city far away. Between S.'s bookcase, wide and deep, still a mysterious temple of wisdom, and my small monk's bed, there is just enough room for me to kneel down. Something I have been wanting to write down for days, perhaps weeks, but which a sort of shyness — or perhaps false shame? — has prevented

---

18. Referring to Han Wegerif, whom she served as housekeeper.

me from putting into words. A desire to kneel down sometimes pulses through my body, or rather it is as if my body had been meant and made for the act of kneeling. Sometimes, in moments of deep gratitude, kneeling down becomes an overwhelming urge, head deeply bowed, hands before my face. It has become a gesture embedded in my body, needing to be expressed from time to time. And I remember: "The girl who could not kneel," and the rough coconut matting in the bathroom. When I write these things down, I still feel a little ashamed, as if I were writing about the most intimate of intimate matters. Much more bashful than if I had to write about my love life. But is there indeed anything as intimate as man's relationship to God? Some distaste because of this about that recent Oxford meeting.[19] So exhibitionist. Such public love-making with God. So bacchanalian, and then all those pious petty-bourgeois men and old spinsters on the lookout for a man. No! Never again. Perhaps it's all right just once, for the experience. But they are too well meaning for one to watch the whole thing as one might a stage play. — April 3, 1942, Good Friday morning, 8:30 a.m.

The threat grows ever greater, and terror increases from day to day. I draw prayer around me like a dark protective wall, withdraw inside it as one might into a convent cell and then step outside again, calmer and stronger and more collected.

---

19. The Oxford Club was a Christian revivalist movement, founded by the American Lutheran pastor and evangelist Frank Buchman (1878–1961) at Oxford, England. Begun in the late 1920s, this movement spread to continental Europe, Asia, and the United States. Usually on weekends, members held so-called house parties, marked by the practices of individual oral confession to the group, hymn singing, group prayer, motivational talks, testimonies of members who had applied spiritual principles to daily life, and a sense of mutual belonging and confidentiality. According to Buchman, the four pillars of Christian behavior were perfect love, perfect selflessness, perfect honesty, and perfect purity, and members were expected to practice them. The founders of Alcoholics Anonymous were inspired by Buchman's four pillars and upon meeting with leaders of the Oxford Club in New York incorporated these into their twelve-step program. Probably at Tide's invitation Etty had attended one of the house parties.

Withdrawing into the closed cell of prayer is becoming an ever-greater reality for me as well as a necessity. That inner concentration erects high walls around me within which I can find my way back to myself, gather myself together into one whole, away from all distractions. I can imagine times to come when I shall stay on my knees for days on end waiting until the protective walls are strong enough to prevent my going to pieces altogether, my being lost and utterly devastated.

— May 18, 1942, Monday

"It is sometimes hard to take in and comprehend, oh God, what those created in Your likeness do to each other in these disjointed days. But I no longer shut myself away in my room, God; I try to look things straight in the face, even the worst crimes, and to discover the small, naked human being amid the monstrous wreckage caused by man's senseless deeds. I don't sit here in my peaceful flower-filled room, praising You through Your poets and thinkers. That would be too simple, and in any case I am not as unworldly as my friends so kindly think. Every human being has his own reality, I know that, but I am no fanciful visionary, God, no schoolgirl with a 'beautiful soul' (Werner said of my novel: 'from a beautiful soul to a great soul'[20]). I try to face up to Your world, God, not to escape from reality into beautiful dreams — though I believe that beautiful dreams can exist beside the most horrible reality — and I continue to praise Your creation, God, despite everything."

— May 29, 1942, Friday morning, 11:30 a.m.

This morning I suddenly had to kneel down on the rough coconut matting in the bathroom, my head bowed so low that it nearly rested in my lap. I could remain like that for days, my body like the safe walls of a small cell sheltering me right in its

---

20. Meaning from Etty to Spier.

middle. I am growing a bit calmer now. Perhaps they will drive us so far that it will feel like merciful relief to be locked up and to have no more daily cares and responsibilities. Then all the responsibility will be theirs. One has to live through these depressions too; one must have no illusions about the world we live in. — July 4, 1942, Saturday morning, 9:00 a.m.

"Dear God, these are anxious times. Tonight for the first time I lay in the dark with burning eyes as scene after scene of human suffering passed before me. I shall promise You one thing, God, just one very small thing: I shall never burden my today with cares about tomorrow, although that takes some practice. Each day is sufficient unto itself.[21] I shall try to help You, God, to stop my strength ebbing away, though I cannot vouch for it in advance. But one thing is becoming increasingly clear to me: that You cannot help us, that we help You to help ourselves. And that is all we can manage these days and also all that really matters: that we safeguard that little of You, God, in ourselves. And perhaps in others as well. Alas, there doesn't seem to be much You Yourself can do about our circumstances, about our lives. Neither do I hold You responsible. You cannot help us, but we must help You and defend Your dwelling place inside us to the last. There are, it is true, some who, even at this late stage, are putting their vacuum cleaners and silver forks and spoons in safekeeping instead of guarding You, dear God. And there are those who want to put their bodies in safekeeping but who are nothing more now than a shelter for a thousand fears and bitter feelings. And they say, 'I shan't let them get me into their clutches.' But they forget that no one is in their clutches who is in Your arms. I am beginning to feel a little more peaceful, God, thanks to this conversation with You. I shall have many more conversations with You. You are sure to go through

---

21. In reference to Matthew 6:34.

lean times with me now and then, when my faith weakens a little, but believe me, I shall always labor for You and remain faithful to You, and I shall never drive You from my presence.

"I have strength enough, God, for suffering on a grand scale, but there are more than a thousand everyday cares that leap up on me without warning like so many fleas. So for the moment I scratch away and tell myself, 'This day has been taken care of now, the protective walls of a hospitable home still surround me like a well-worn, familiar piece of clothing, there is food enough for today, and the bed with the white sheets and the warm blankets stands waiting for me tonight, so don't let me waste even one atom of my strength on petty material cares. Let me use and spend every minute and turn this into a fruitful day, one stone more in the foundations on which to build our so uncertain future.' "

The jasmine behind my house has been completely ruined by the rains and storms of the last few days; its white blossoms are floating about in muddy black pools on the low garage roof. But somewhere inside me the jasmine continues to blossom undisturbed, just as profusely and delicately as ever it did. And it spreads its scent round the House in which You dwell, oh God. You can see, I look after You, I bring You not only my tears and my forebodings on this stormy, gray Sunday morning, I even bring you scented jasmine. And I shall bring You all the flowers I shall meet on my way, and truly there are many of those. I shall try to make You at home always. Even if I should be locked up in a narrow cell and a cloud should drift past my small barred window, then I shall bring you that cloud, oh God, while there is still the strength in me to do so. I cannot promise You anything for tomorrow, but my intentions are good, You can see.

And now I shall venture out upon this day, I shall meet a great many people today, and evil rumors and threats will again assault me like so many enemy soldiers besieging an inviolable fortress.

— July 12, 1942 [entry is titled "Sunday morning prayer"]

SOLITUDE, SILENCE, AND DETACHMENT

Solitude and silence allow for detaching from the outside world so as to better hear one's inner voice. Etty comes to experience that in solitude and silence she can discern God's dynamic presence in her. She guards this interior space against the natural human desire to depend on others, outer circumstances, the outside world. Comparing her solitude to a monastic "cell," she longs for a convent-like structure that would protect her from din and noise and outside interference. Etty's allusions to a monastic environment may be largely due to the books she is reading: works by Christian monastics and mystics as well as the novels of Dostoevsky. Detailed descriptions of monastic life are also found in Rainer Maria Rilke's The Book of Hours *(1905), a three-part series of continuous intimate prayers addressing God and written as if by a Russian monk turned painter and iconographer. Etty frequently quotes from this book in her diaries and had taken it with her to Westerbork, where, along with the Bible, she kept it under her pillow. The themes of solitude and silence figure prominently in Etty's writing, as does the mystical practice of detachment, severing emotional attachments and shedding the desire to possess others. By these practices, she is able to better discern her inner melody, the central interior tune sounded in the place where God dwells. She struggles with attachments to others, especially Spier, since they disrupt the "hearkening" to herself and discerning the soul's and God's dynamic presence at her center. Keeping a diary forces upon her solitude and silence and permits her to step back and take an honest look at herself. Later, she is able to practice solitude even in a noisy crowd by pulling away internally and, as a result, perceiving the continuous flow of life and its growth within her as one interconnected whole.*

One person should never make another the center of his life.

I must bear this in mind at all times. If you are tied to another he will absorb your strength, with the result that you have less to give to him. One must be a world all of one's own, with one's own center, and from that center one can then transmit beams of forces or what have you to others.

Yesterday I was stuck to S. And I felt my strength fail. As a result I was unable to be as intensely involved with him as I normally am. I also had too much of a physical longing for him. And though, deep down, my longing for him was not really erotic, I have gradually developed such warm feelings for him that I felt the need to be very close. Still, I longed more for the human being than for the man. It was really the first time that I did not see him as a highly sensual man, and that I did not come away from his arms feeling lonely. But there is also the immediate danger of growing too attached to him, as well as the realization that I must struggle free of him, that I must live my own life — I am still at the beginning of mine while he has already entered upon his final stage. I have to cut through all the threads that keep growing between him and me every time we meet. It costs me a lot of pain and takes a great deal of strength, but if I can fight this fight to the end, I shall be stronger than ever before.   — June 9, 1941, Monday morning, 9:30 a.m.

More arrests, more terror, concentration camps, the arbitrary dragging off of fathers, sisters, brothers. We seek the meaning of life, wondering whether any meaning can be left. But that is something each one of us must settle with himself and with God. And perhaps life has its own meaning, even if it takes a lifetime to find it. I for one have ceased to cling to life and to things; I have the feeling that everything is accidental, that one must break one's inner bonds with people and stand aside for all else. Everything seems so menacing and ominous, and always that feeling of total impotence.

— June 14, 1941, Saturday, 7:00 p.m.

We are but hollow vessels, washed through by history.

Everything is chance, or nothing is chance. If I believed the first, I would be unable to live on, but I am not yet fully convinced of the second.

I have become just a little stronger again. I can fight things out within myself. Your first impulse is always to get help from others, to think you can't make it, but then suddenly you notice that you've fought your way through and that you've pulled it off all by yourself, and that makes you stronger. Last Sunday (was it only a week ago?) I had the desperate feeling that I was tied to him and that because of that I was in for an utterly miserable time. But I pulled myself out of it, although I don't quite know how. Not by arguing it out with myself, but by tugging with all my mental strength at some imaginary rope. I threw all my weight behind it and stood my ground, and suddenly I felt that I was free again. And then there were those brief meetings (in the evening at the bench on the Stadion-kade, shopping in town) that were of an intensity that, for me at least, was greater than anything before. It was all thanks to that lack of attachment; all my love and sympathy and concern and happiness went out to him, but I made no more demands on him, I wanted nothing from him, I took him as he was and enjoyed him.

I'd just like to know how I did it, how I managed to break free. If I knew that, as I really should, then I might perhaps be able to help others with the same problems. Perhaps it is like a man tied to another with a rope and tugging until he breaks loose. He, too, probably won't be able to tell just how he did it;

all he does know is that he managed to get away, that he had the *will* to do so, and that he struggled with all his might. That's what must have happened inside me.

And the lesson I learned is this: thought doesn't help; what you need is not causal explanation but will and a great deal of mental energy.   —June 15, 1941, Sunday, noon

I know two sorts of loneliness. One makes me feel dreadfully unhappy, lost and forlorn, the other makes me feel strong and happy. The first always appears when I feel out of touch with my fellow men, with everything, when I am completely cut off from others and from myself and can see no purpose in life or any connection between things, nor have the slightest idea where I fit in. With the other kind of loneliness, by contrast, I feel very strong and certain and connected with everyone and everything and with God, and realize that I can manage on my own and that I am not dependent upon others. Then I know that I am part of a meaningful whole and that I can impart a great deal of strength to others.

The first kind of loneliness is the dangerous one. It is the one I have to stand up to. It comes from my still lacking the courage to be myself and to face the world. And that letter from S. yesterday was so important. At first I felt quite divorced from it, cut off even from S. Then I flung myself onto my bed. I lay there on my back, and suddenly a number of crucial and productive thoughts came to me. And I was again flooded with life and warmth, and felt so close to that dear, good person. My sickness is that ultimately every human being remains a stranger to me, does not really take permanent root in my heart. Yesterday he was suddenly much less of a stranger. I felt that this was a serious matter and that I had to treat it with due seriousness.

One human being must not be the end of another but the means. The means of reaching a higher stage of life. The means of breaking free of this much too burdensome earth and its creatures. With one another and through one another we must learn to free ourselves from one another and to live together in a higher freedom. That is well meant, but not yet well said. It takes a whole lifetime to experience these things clearly and distinctly and then to formulate them so lucidly that someone else can derive some benefit from them. There is that cork bottling me up again. And yet, today, I am a bit further on than I was yesterday, although that same old headache is back and the same old first twinges of a stomachache. But still, I have grown quite a bit, I have tilled a little bit more land, although vast tracts still lie fallow. What causes me the greatest pain is my continued inability to say things, to express them in such a way that the words become transparent and the spirit behind them can be seen. That's laying it on much too thick, my girl.

— August 9, 1941, Saturday, 3:00 p.m.

What I do is *hineinhorchen* ("to hearken to"; it seems to me that this word is untranslatable). Hearkening to myself, to others, to the world. I listen very intently, with my whole being, and try to fathom the meaning of things. I am always very tense and attentive, I keep looking for something but don't know what. What I am looking for, of course, is my own truth, but I still have no idea what it will look like. I go blindly after a certain objective, I can feel there is an objective, but where and how I do not know.

— August 23, 1941, Saturday night behind the desk

Sometimes I feel that every word spoken and every gesture made merely serve to exacerbate misunderstandings. Then what I would really like is to escape into a great silence and impose that silence on everyone else. Yes, every word can aggravate the misunderstanding on this too crowded world.

— October 20, 1941, Monday morning

In the past when I sat at my desk I was always terribly anxious in case I was missing out on "real life." As a result I could never concentrate on my studies. When I was out in "real life," out among people, I would always long gloomily to be back at my desk, and wasn't really happy in their midst. But the artificial division between study and "real life" has now gone. I now truly "live" at my desk. Studying has become a really "live" experience and no longer involves my mind alone. At my desk I am in the midst of life in abundance, and I carry the inner peace and balance I have acquired there into the outside. In the past I had to keep withdrawing from the world because its many impressions confused me and made me unhappy. I would have to escape into a quiet room. Now I carry this "quiet room" inside me, as it were, and can escape into it at any moment — whether sitting in a crowded tram or out on the town.

— January 9, 1942, Friday, 6:00 p.m.

I seem to be achieving a state of complete equilibrium. I no longer have to creep into the corner beside the wardrobe in order to "hearken unto myself." I now listen all day long to what is within me, and even when I am with others I no longer have to withdraw but am able to draw strength from the most deeply hidden sources in myself.

— January 19, 1942, Monday morning, 10:00 a.m.

This morning is all mine. And now that I have made myself sit down quietly, along with this exercise book, I can see what hard going it still is, how much one is governed by restlessness and impatience. Always the same old excuse: I haven't the time, I'm too busy. But all it really comes down to is one's own restlessness. Not allowing the stillness to develop to its fullest extent, but being satisfied with those far too brief moments of peace and introspection which are increasingly being woven into my everyday life. But out of sheer impatience I still stumble over the small intervals of stillness, am much too easily satisfied, delude myself into thinking that I am "hearkening" to myself. But now that, for the first time in weeks, I am making myself say "This morning is all mine," I can see how much impatience and "living for the day" there is still in me. On the third of February I was one year old. I think I'll celebrate February 3 as my birthday from now on — it is more important than January 15, the day my umbilical cord was cut. But I won't go into that here. It seems it happened so long ago, now, that February 3. For days I had no need to write anything down, no need *hineinzuhören* because I was in a constant state of "hearkening to myself." (Why can't I find a decent Dutch equivalent for this expression in German?) I stopped saying my prayers then because I genuinely kept praying inside. At night when I went to bed it was as if the rich harvest of the day lay piled up high in my arms, in almost too much abundance to be embraced. What a good thing that such states do not persist. One has to be jolted from one's own center into a state of unrest time and again in order to regain a greater peace once more. One must never be too certain of anything, for then all growth comes to a halt. But this, too, is not what I wanted to write about this morning.

It isn't always possible to carry words straight from one's solitary and richly contemplative nights into the day. That's something I have noticed as well. How I love you, my solitary nights! I lie stretched out on my back in my narrow bed, completely abandoned to the night — with chilblains, a hot-water bottle, a cold, and a woolen shawl wrapped around my head, but none of that matters. Facing my bed, S.'s large bookcase still stands like a threatening, mysterious temple, the curtain is open, the night is a gray expanse at the window, the Skating Club grounds are a broad, white snowy steppe. I lie there on my back with a sense of how much I am part of a great process of growth. Last night I felt suddenly that my inner landscape was like a ripening cornfield. At night that sounds so simple and true: inside me are cornfields, growing and ripening. But when you try to carry those words across the threshold of the early morning they seem slightly out of place. Last night there was so much I would have liked to bring back with me to write down on these narrow blue lines, but I have realized now that that's far from simple. "Everything is bearing and the giving birth..." "and to await the hour of birth of a new clarity with deep humility and patience."[22]

It is a great deal merely to realize that one comprises part of a great growing process, indeed simply to be aware of such a process. I believe that for far too many people life still consists of rather disconnected, accidental moments.

—February 20, 1942, Friday morning, 10:00 a.m.

This last week has brought clear proof of how much stronger I have become. I keep following my own inner voice even in the madhouse in which I work, with a hundred people chattering together in one small room, typewriters clattering, and me sitting in a corner reading Rilke. Yesterday we were all moved out suddenly in the middle of the morning; tables and chairs were pulled from under us, people thronged about giving orders and counter-orders, even about the smallest chair, but Etty just sat down in a corner on the dirty floor between her typewriter and a packet of sandwiches and read Rilke. I make my own rules and do as I like. In all this chaos and misery I follow my own rhythm, so much so that at any given moment between typing letters I can immerse myself in the things that matter to me. It is not that I am cutting myself off from all the suffering around me, but I go my own way. Yesterday was a silly day. A day in which my sardonic humor asserted itself and I suddenly felt like an exuberant child. God save me from one thing: don't let me

---

22. Quoted from Rilke, *Briefe an einen jungen Dichter* ("Letters to a Young Poet").

be sent to a camp with the people with whom I now work every day. I could write a hundred satires about them....

There is a vast silence in me that continues to grow. And washing around in it are so many words that make one tired because one can express nothing with them. One must do more and more without meaningless words the better to find the few one needs. And in the silence, new powers of expression must grow.

It is now 9:30. I want to sit here at this desk until noon; the rose petals lie scattered among my books. A yellow rose has opened as far as it can and now looks at me large and wide. The two and a half hours I have left seem to me like a year's seclusion. There is a vast silence in me that continues to grow. I am so grateful for these few hours and also for my concentration, which is continuing to grow.

Later...

One day I shall find my own words for the things I have to say; meanwhile I keep borrowing them from Rainer Maria.

"...that actually there are no decisions. That is true. For when one thing follows so naturally, so freely, from another inside you, there is no room left for decision. The chain unwinds, link after link, one attached to the other, lightly yet firmly clasped, movable and yet in unending association."[23]

— July 25, 1942, Saturday morning, 9:00 a.m.

---

23. Quoted from Rilke, *Briefe 1907–1914*.

2

The World

THE SINGLE LIFE

In religious traditions a commitment to the single life usually involves a vow of celibacy, abstaining from sexual relations. This vow is expected of members of monastic orders and some religious leaders and is made in front of a faith community during a liturgical ceremony. Lay members, on the other hand, may make a commitment to remain single directly to God or another person. The reason for such a commitment is to ensure single-hearted devotion to God and sufficient freedom in remaining focused and available to many people. Since Etty never had the desire for children, marriage to her appears as a constraint that prevents women from becoming truly human and engaged in sharing their gifts with all of humanity. Rilke's own commitment to the single life[1] inspires and affirms her. She wonders whether it is truly possible for a woman to remain single without violating her essential nature as woman. She concludes that

---

1. Rilke married the sculptor Clara Westhoff in April 1901 and they had a daughter, Ruth, born the same year. Within a year of marriage the couple split, largely at Rilke's request in order to allow him to pursue his work and art and presumably allowing Clara to pursue hers. They remained on friendly terms. Though they never formally divorced due to scarce finances and legal difficulties, the marital relationship ended with their separation.

*it is but will require enormous effort on the woman's part. Etty
makes that effort. Still, the tension persists between her strong
emotional and erotic attachment to Spier and the fact that he is
unobtainable, the spiritual kinship she senses with him and the
freedom she enjoys during times of emotional distancing from
him. Though Etty lives under Wegerif's roof and has with him a
noncommittal intimate relationship, her internal struggles result
from her attachment to Spier. In time, Rilke's writings help her
to bear the longing for physical union with Spier and to displace
and transcend this longing for the sake of a "higher" cause.
Her decision in early July to volunteer working for the Jewish
Council marks her resolve to live a single life for the sake of
others and God. In a turn of irony, it is then that the opportunity presents itself for her to marry Spier in a spurious legal
arrangement intended to protect him from deportation by the
Nazi authorities. Spier dies before the plan can be carried out.*

Etty, I have something very serious to point out to you. You
think you are obsessed by his mouth, his eyes, his whole body,
and that you cannot rid yourself of them. But make no mis-
take. You rake it all over time and again in your imagination in
order to revel in it. In a way you want him to obsess you and to
pursue you physically, because you like it. You have become so
used all your life to getting your hands on men in your imagination, and in the most shameless manner, that it has become a
habit and is hard to break so suddenly. But you must be well
aware, my girl, that if you really don't want anything from
him, then it doesn't need to happen. Still, you are like a child
with a favorite plaything, bringing it out all the time to enjoy
it and play with it some more. And that is what you are doing
with S. You deliberately keep conjuring him up in your mind,
which is not surprising as one doesn't often come across anyone as fascinating. And the fact that he, too, is on the point
of entering into a relationship with you makes him even more

attractive. He has now come within your reach, and that rather flatters your vanity, and on top of that there is also something very base, very earthy and "acquisitive" about it: all this can be mine, that mouth, those hands, those eyes, and if I am honest — this paper will keep the secret — there is also the feeling that it would be a sin to let all this go by the board, that I should be sorry later to have turned him down when I shall probably never again meet such a man. And don't forget that you are a "challenge" for him as well, as he himself has said. For two years a man with his temperament has lived without a woman, has tried to remain faithful to his "lonely girlfriend waiting in London." And I would be destroying that fidelity; far better if I joined his fight to preserve it. I too have a relationship, after all. I love Han with a good and pure and deep affection; I should not want to do without him in my life. A person should not try to have everything, not even if he can get it. If I can really win this struggle, then I will have grown that much stronger and shall probably have achieved something worthwhile for the first time in my life. Yesterday his face was still a beloved landscape, dim but omnipresent in the background. Now nothing is dim any longer, I can see those bright eyes clearly, with their sometimes incredibly impish look, and that expressive mouth, mobile and full of deep emotion, indeed this afternoon that whole lively face, sparkling with wit, had suddenly lost much of its usual gravity and was twinkling with charm — poor Etty, you really have got it bad. But you must apply your will, and I am not convinced that you really know what you want. The tensions, of course, are always tugging hard in the background, yet there can be a close human relationship despite those tensions *without having an affair.* But though I have been getting so much off my chest, I have a terribly tense feeling in my head and my cheeks are burning. I am going to stretch out now on the hearth rug, do some breathing exercises, and try to work up some courage. The tension does not arise from my longing for him but purely and simply from my not yet being a hundred percent certain that I don't want to have an affair with him — there are always a few percent that do. Though I have built a solid structure of will power in my imagination, I have left a small back door open, with the result that the building is not as solid as it could be, and that is why I feel so tense and agitated. It is best to be as clear in one's mind as possible about that.

How silly, I keep reaching for this exercise book to add a bit more. My main weakness, in fact, is that all the time, or, at least very often, I am plagued by the great big question, which is actually a void: Is the struggle really worth the effort? Is it worthwhile putting up a fight? Shouldn't one just be taking what life has to offer and leave it at that? There is probably an even more banal question behind that one: who will thank you for putting up a fight, or, quite bluntly, who will give two pins? God will, no doubt, and these words suddenly pouring from my small fountain pen fill me directly with humble strength. Perhaps these words — God will thank you for it — will turn into my salvation.   — March 19, 1941, Wednesday, 9:00 p.m.

He said that love of mankind is greater than love of one man. For when you love one person you are merely loving yourself.

He is a mature fifty-five-year-old and has reached the stage where he can love all mankind, having loved many individuals in the past. I am an ordinary twenty-seven-year-old girl, and I too am filled with love for all mankind, but for all I know I shall always continue to be in search of my one man. And I wonder to what extent that is a handicap, a woman's handicap. Whether it is an ancient tradition from which she must liberate herself, or whether it is so much part of her very essence that she would be doing violence to herself if she bestowed her love on all mankind instead of on a single man. (I can't yet see how the two can be combined.) Perhaps that's why there are so few famous women scientists and artists: a woman always looks for the one man on whom she can bestow all her wisdom, warmth, love, and creative powers. She longs for a man, not for mankind....

Perhaps the true, the essential emancipation of women still has to come. We are not yet full human beings; we are the "weaker sex." We are still tied down and enmeshed in centuries-old traditions. We still have to be born as human beings; that is the great task that lies before us.

— August 4, 1941, Monday, 2:30 p.m.

Yes, we women, we foolish, idiotic, illogical women, we all seek Paradise and the Absolute. And yet my brain, my capable brain, tells me that there are no absolutes, that everything is relative, endlessly diverse, and in eternal motion, and that it is precisely for that reason that life is so exciting and fascinating, but also so very, very painful. We women want to perpetuate ourselves in a man.

— September 25, 1941, Thursday morning, 9:00 a.m.

Yesterday I felt like screaming out loud in this exercise book: I want a man, a man all to myself. One does have such moments. Actually, I want nothing of the kind. I feel I must try to do so many things in this life. I sometimes long for a man as a definition, a demarcation of my own being, because I am afraid of losing myself in space with a center unknown to me. But my center must lie in myself, deep in myself, that is the only thing that matters. I don't know about other women. Well, and now for my daily program, it isn't all that much — teaching Russian for an hour and this evening chirology, and, of course, the dentist. The program oppresses me dreadfully today, but it's no good philosophizing about it; I must simply get down to following it. — October 3, 1941, Friday morning, 9:00 a.m.

On the way to Tide, between the Skating Club and Euterpe-straat, I suddenly had the feeling that Hertha[2] was coming back. My heart broke in those few streets several times over. I waged a heroic struggle and then took off for faraway Russia, after first having written him a heartrending letter to tell him I was but a frail human being who could not cope with him and Hertha combined. Nor did I want to have anything more to do with his work, and I suddenly puzzled hard whether I had not chosen the work for the man's sake rather than the man for his work's sake. And though I knew that I would never want to marry him, I could not put up with his having another woman. The whole business made me feel quite dreadful, and it went on for several streets. I got to Tide's feeling leaden and sad, but once there I immediately launched into the fascinating land-scape of the palm of her hand and noticed how much I was back in the grip of the subject and how much pleasure it gave me. And when I saw that Wiep was gloomy and down in the dumps, she suddenly had all my attention, and my own sadness was completely gone. That often happens to me — when I see that others are sad, my own spirits recover and I feel like cry-ing out, "Look, it really isn't all that bad, it will pass, you are taking it much harder than you need to...."

To sum up:

I shall certainly be able to get over Hertha's coming here and be able to cope with it, though it may take a bit of a struggle, and that is something I am starting on right now.

If I see that somebody else is sad, I forget my own sadness and try to understand and help the other.

Life is beautiful, even though I am again teetering danger-ously on the verge of depression and chaos.

— October 3, 1941, Friday, 11:00 p.m.

---

2. Hertha Levi, Spier's fiancée, who lived in London.

It is a slow and painful process, this striving after true inner freedom. Growing more and more certain that there is no help or assurance or refuge in others. That the others are just as uncertain and weak and helpless as you are. You are always thrown back on to your own resources. There is nothing else. The rest is make-believe. But that fact has to be recognized over and over again. Especially since you are a woman. For woman always longs to lose herself in another. But that too is a fiction, albeit a beautiful one. There is no matching of lives. At least not for me. Perhaps for a few moments. But do those moments justify a lifetime together? Can those few moments cement a shared existence? All they can do is give you a little strength. And perhaps a little happiness. God knows, being alone is hard. For the world is inhospitable.

My heart runs quite wild, but never for just one person. For all mankind. I believe this heart of mine is very rich indeed. In the past I used to dream of giving it to one person. But it was not to be. And when you reach such painful truths at the age of twenty-seven, you sometimes feel quite desperate and lonely and *anxious,* although independent and proud at the same time. I have confidence in myself; and I shall manage by myself. The only measure you have is yourself. And the only responsibility you can shoulder in life is responsibility for yourself. But you must do it with all your strength. And now to ring up S....

To S. during a late telephone call:
"I would sooner sleep with books than with men." "That is a giant step forward." And to Han, "No, don't lead me into temptation; I really must go to sleep." And Han, quick to take offense, "Temptation, indeed! Go sleep with your books!"[3]
— October 21, 1941, Tuesday, after dinner

---

3. Etty later lightly crossed out this passage with a pen and wrote: "19-12-42, / common and vulgar / Shame on you, Etty, were you like that."

Yesterday I kissed S.'s hair, which is getting quite gray over his right temple. But his neck is still so young. I love him with a love that tries to be less and less possessive and hence possesses more and more. Now and then there are still petty jealousies, outbursts, dissatisfaction, and a terrible longing. That is all to the good. Otherwise you might almost think you were a saint.

— February 20, 1942, Friday morning, 10:00 a.m.

I am very angry with him. I so want to be in his arms. I think it is so mean of him to leave me so shriveled up; it makes me feel very rebellious, yet apathetic at the same time. Right now I'm not even able to say that I love him. Everything seems so confused. Desire is "making itself at home" in me, spreading out and taking over my entire inner life and weighing me down like lead.

It is half past eight. Han is lying in bed, a coughing, wheezing old man with kind blue eyes. Everything's a bit depressing. My body feels so young and so lonely and betrayed. There isn't a single kind thought in me, I'm miserable and I hate everybody. It hadn't yet reached that point this morning and wasn't like that at all yesterday. Then I enjoyed a carefree spring afternoon with Alice Levie. But this afternoon, when I saw S. again, it suddenly came over me.

— March 1, 1942, Sunday night, 8:30 p.m.

Oh yes, and this occurred to me last night as well: in such moods of spring fever one is inclined to look on one's erotic and sexual desire as the very center of one's being. But suddenly I realized once again: no matter how dominant it may appear to be, it is only a part, no more than a part. And it was very clear in my mind that the writing of a small piece of prose, or a conversation about fundamental life-and-death matters with a fellow human being, will always give me greater and more lasting satisfaction than a marriage bed. And because that was so clear in my mind, despite my tormenting desire, my harmony was nearly restored. We should always remember that we are made up of a multiplicity of parts, and though we may occasionally allow ourselves to be carried away by just one — and that too has its appeal — most people allow themselves to be so dominated and carried away by that one part that their entire life is distorted and thrown off balance.

— March 2, 1942, Monday morning, 8:00 a.m.

Become an instrument, not only in your spirit but in your body as well. This is, of course, being written under the influence of Rilke, of Rainer Maria, who has been there as large as life in the midst of my life these past few weeks and who is becoming a more and more powerful support for the tender shoots that are about to spring gingerly to life within me. Under Rilke's influence, yet genuinely from within myself. The foreign lands to which I shall be going — I know that more and more surely — a youthful restlessness that is turning into certainty and the many people's faces which will be as so many landscapes over which I shall travel. I still have to learn my languages better, and then I must listen, listen everywhere, listen to the very essence of things. And love, and take my leave and by so doing die, but be reborn, everything so painful and yet so full of life. — I am twenty-eight years old. Sometimes I think that is ancient, and yet I am only just beginning.

Tonight's experience: the *Duino Elegies* and some of the letters from Muzot.[4]

I had not given this day up for lost at the start, and it lifted itself up and proffered me this full and flourishing ending once more. Night after night I retire to bed, my heart replenished with gratitude. The intense association with Rilke these last few days still weighs so heavily on me that my own words cannot

---

4. Both the *Duino Elegies* and the letters are by Rilke.

break free from under it. I ought to have written a great deal to S. This, too, was a new achievement last week: "You must not seek a hundred small satisfactions for one great longing, you must keep it whole, raise it to a higher plane as it were, and draw strength and inspiration from it for loving many people." "But that is so hard at times."

However: "Longing, after all, is always greater than its satisfaction. And that is probably how it ought to be."

Time and again I bring the exercise book out of my drawer, just to add another verse. Shall I experience these lines as intensely later on as I experience them now?

A few lines from Rilke's "All Things Almost Do Call Us to Connect":

> ... Through every creature one great space extends
> as outer space within. And birds fly silently
> Through us. And I who wants to grow look outward
> but to find that *in* me grows the tree.[5]

— March 8, 1942, Sunday, 10:00 p.m.

Suddenly it surfaces in me again as an ever greater certainty: I shall never marry. Never divide the great Longing into a host of small satisfactions. Perhaps it will find, just once, great and unsullied, a safe haven, a single night of love, and after that one must bear one's Longing large and undivided within one, draw strength from it to love everyone and not just one's own small satisfactions.

"One must not divide one's great longing into a hundred small satisfactions."

And now, good night.

— March 8, 1942, Sunday, 11:00 p.m.
in the bathroom with cold cream on my face

---

5. From Rilke, *Gedichte 1906–26* ("Poems 1906–26").

THE DISCIPLINE OF WORK

Work, when not used as an end in itself or idol, can be a discipline of forgetting oneself while finding one's true self in the process. Such self-forgetfulness through work can be an act of worship and service to God. The healing effects of labor are emphasized by the oldest monastic rule of the West, the Rule of St. Benedict, where monks and nuns alternate between set times of prayer and labor, "ora et labora." Thus, the work of common people was given spiritual value, as opposed to only the work of members of a religious order. Later a seeming juxtaposition evolved between work and worship that was reconciled by such reformers as Ignatius of Loyola, whose incarnational spirituality saw in work and its diligent pursuit and execution a means of worship and praise aimed at the greater glory of God. Etty discovers that work, regardless of how menial, can be a spiritual discipline to help her draw closer to God. By concentrating on the task at hand, she gains a sense of self-forgetfulness, a sense of inner harmony and peace, a feeling of being at one with herself and God. While never a particularly good student in high school or college, she begins appreciating the spiritual benefit of faithfully tackling the daily tasks. The tasks she assumes are keeping a diary, doing her Russian translations, preparing for Russian class and giving lessons, and working on her inner self. She becomes more serious about doing her housework and is even willing to seek additional employment as a housekeeper or companion. Working for Spier, however, is fraught with tension: she enjoys the regular contact with him and learning about the field of helping others but is also burdened by her romantic attachment, rekindled with each contact. Eventually, she begins to accept the burdens and demands of each type of work. What were previously considered interruptions and intrusions on her time of writing, reading, and finding herself, she can now welcome as

*opportunities for spiritual growth, increased awareness of self,
and ever new ways of discerning God's presence.*

You never get something for nothing. Severe inner tension. Difficult. Behind Lermontov[6] there inevitably looms S.'s gray, lined face, the way he sat there yesterday at the table, withdrawn into himself, clenched strength, intelligent eyes looking out of that warm strength, that private, fascinating world that he is. Oh dear, this all looks a bit too much like fine writing, but all I did was scribble it down; it seems best to me to just let it come off the pen. And that is the difficulty with the work. I'm always wanting to go to that dear face, talk to him, stroke him, busy myself with him in my imagination, but I thrust him away, swear like a navvy, it simply must not happen, it really mustn't, I have work to do, and I actually manage finally, with great concentration, to study a Lermontov poem. Working with concentration is the most wonderful thing there is, but heavens above, how much of a struggle it still entails. And now off to class. My attitude to it has changed. In the past, that's to say last week, I still half listened and half dreamed and kept thinking, oh well, I'll go over what he says later on, but first let me indulge in these lovely fantasies. Downright shameful, feeble and awful — for as long as you go on being so half-hearted, nothing will come of it. But now you shall pay attention. You must *will* it! Everything hinges on that.
— March 11, 1941, Tuesday morning, 10:30 a.m.

You mustn't keep asking yourself how you are feeling now; you must simply get down to work. Then one fine day the work will take the place of your feeling out of sorts, which is how it ought to be....

---

6. Michail Yuryevich Lermontov (1814–41) was a Russian poet and writer.

Anyone who tackles an important task must forget himself. Under this motto I have entrusted myself to S. The word "important" is something I need not apply to myself for the time being, although I have a strong suspicion that, were I to forget myself, I might yet achieve something of importance. But in fact that is something I ought not to be concerned about either, something that will become clear, and the character of my future work will depend on how I conduct myself towards my work today. Above all, I must not have any fantasies about the future, I must not even think this morning what it will be like at S.'s this afternoon. That is the only way of experiencing reality intensely and absolutely, untroubled by thoughts ahead, which are bound not to correspond with reality, and do nothing but disillusion, tire and confuse one.

But now: Church Slavonic.[7] Somehow I must learn to roll back the barrier. I simply cannot find an explanation for the awful inhibition I have towards this part of my work. For months I have been sitting there just staring at it, and whenever I finally make up my mind to take up that old Bulgarian once more, I get something like a lump in my throat and palpitations and so much antipathy and anxiety that I quickly go and start something else and fob myself off with promises that I'll start "tomorrow." And so it goes on for months on end. But now, my girl, all that messing about must finally stop. The sermon starts as follows: you may not so much as ask yourself whether or not you like the subject *or whether or not you see any sense in it;* it is part of your studies, of the work you have chosen, so it's absolutely no good wondering whether you should do it tomorrow, or the day after, or "some day." No, you are going to get down to it today.

---

7. Old Church Slavonic, or what Etty calls old Bulgarian, was the earliest written language of the Slavs.

So now I reach gingerly for my lecture notes, and it is as if I have had to roll back heavy granite boulders, but I *shall* make a start straightaway. And if I should really manage to get back into the subject, and return to Van Wijk in Leiden,[8] then that would be one of the most brilliant things S. would have done for me so far.　　　— March 12, 1941, Wednesday, 9:00 a.m.

Amsterdam, March 16, 1941

Dear Madam,

In response to your advertisement in the Handelsblad of March 15, I take the liberty of informing you that:

I am a student of literature, aged twenty-seven, thus a mature student, having earlier been engaged in various other fields.

For some time now I have been looking for part-time employment, preferably not of an intellectual kind.

I was struck by your advertisement because I felt it would make a pleasant change from my intellectual exertions to keep somebody company and offer them companionship.

I would add that for some years now I have been paying for my board and lodging by providing good cheer and companionship to a family who also employ a housekeeper.

I look forward to hearing from you in due course.

Yours faithfully,

My life's priorities have been suddenly changed. In the past, I liked to start the day on an empty stomach with Dostoevsky and Hegel, and during odd, jumpy moments I might also darn a

---

8. Nikolaas van Wijk (1880–1941) was a scholar of Dutch and Slavonic languages, the founder of Baltic and Slavonic Studies in the Netherlands, and a scholar of international reputation. He held the only chair on the subject in the Netherlands before 1945, a chair at the University of Leiden. When the university closed in November 1940, students were welcome to ask van Wijk for individual support and lessons.

stocking if I absolutely had to. Now I start the day, in the most literal sense, with the stocking and gradually work my way up through the other essential chores to higher planes, where I can meet poets and philosophers again.

I shall have to sweat blood to rid my style of all that pathos if I am ever to make anything of it, but really it's all a matter of looking for the right words.

—March 16, 1941, Sunday morning, 11:00 a.m.

They ate themselves to a standstill and clung ever more firmly to solid earth. This following a tomato sandwich, one apple syrup sandwich, and three cups of tea with real sugar. I tend to toy with asceticism, to think I would love to brave hunger and thirst, cold and heat. But it's all romantic nonsense, for as soon as it gets the least bit cold what I like best is to crawl into bed and not get out again.

Last night I told S. that all those books are really bad for me, some of them, anyway. That they make me lazy and passive, and I want to do nothing but read. I only remember one word from his reply: "corruption."

Sometimes it takes so much effort to get through the daily round — getting up, washing, exercises, putting on stockings without holes, laying the table, in short getting through the basics — that little is left over for other things. Yet when, like any other decent citizen, I get up on time, I feel proudly that I have achieved something marvelous. That's what I need desperately: discipline from without as long as my inner discipline is still so imperfect. If I stay in bed an extra hour in the morning, it doesn't mean I need more sleep, but simply that I'm unable to cope....

Do whatever your hand finds to do and don't take thought for the morrow. Make your bed and carry your dirty cups to the kitchen and face the rest as it comes. Get Tide some sunflowers today, prepare *Gore ut uma,*[9] teach that teenage girl some Russian pronunciation, and work the schizoid tendencies that elude your psychological powers of understanding out of your system. Do whatever your hand and spirit find to do, live every hour to the full, and stop fussing about with your thoughts and fears. I shall have to take your education in hand once again, my girl.　　— October 20, 1941, Monday morning

Terrible antipathy towards the work at S.'s. The feeling that I am wasting my time, that it's all nonsense. Conscious arguments against that feeling: look upon the work as a nice little job, something that's earning you some money, even if not very much; you never know what it might be good for, and it's interesting as well. Truly formidable antipathy. A feeling of: I don't need this. Stomachache as well. A sense of frustration. Can't face anything. Even the Russian lesson I've got to give tomorrow.

Last night it was just the other way around: a high point. Read Pfister's *Psychoanalysis and Philosophy.* Was able to get right into it and to get a lot out of it, and I thought with gratitude of S., of how much the broadening of my horizon is due to him, due to personal contact with him but also to the psychological work done with him. Sincere, honest gratitude and love for him.

Now, great antipathy. We shall have to face up to it squarely for once. Take a good look at it when the enthusiasm comes back.
　　— November 21, 1941, Friday

One more flicker before I drop off.

It's true, I'm quite sure of it: I work very hard. My nearest and dearest would laugh if they heard this, but inside me, inside

---

9. Title of a play translated as "The Misfortune of Being Clever" by the Russian playwright Alexander Sergeyevich Griboyedov (1795–1829).

my brain, there is an enormous workshop where fashioning, forging, laboring, suffering and sweating all go on. But what the end product may be I do not know. It isn't just vague dreaming. Something is demanding to be given shape. Something is at work, and at moments like this I accept it without demur.

"Cast life aside as something too hard to handle," I scribbled this morning on a piece of paper. That strikes me as a cheap and irresponsible statement now. I know that I shall have to live my life to the full come what may. And my inner workshop must never be closed; I have to keep it at the ready.

—November 22, 1941, Saturday evening

Well, I'm just not going to do it. It's chronic self-violation. I am not going to do any more chirology, and that's that. I am just incapable of doing that sort of thing. Having some knowledge of the technique will still be a help because I'll be able to follow his argument somewhat better.

Just telephoned that childish Indian ayah[10] to say I haven't got any spare time. That shows I mean business, doesn't it? A person simply mustn't allow herself to be put off course. Not even to earn an extra fifteen guilders. Best to confine myself to just one field. I'll be happy to be his secretary, and the psychological aspect does interest me. But for the rest it's over. And now for Karl Nötzel's *Contemporary Russia*.

I suddenly realized with equal clarity that business correspondence isn't for me either.

No more so than chirology. Psychology, yes, but then in a purely theoretical way and as a tool for getting closer to literature. What a pity that lady suddenly sounded so sad over the telephone. But there you are. It wouldn't matter to me if I had to earn my living washing dishes one day, doing something in

---

10. Possibly the woman who had advertised for a companion in the paper and to whose employment ad Etty had responded.

which I am not emotionally involved, so long as I also had a field of study of my own.

It is honestly a relief and it isn't laziness on my part, but the whole thing was getting too stupid. I'm curious about how I'm going to put it to S.

—November 24, 1941, Monday morning, 11:30 a.m.

Look, God, I'll do my best. I shall not withdraw from life. I shall stay down here and try to develop any talents I may have. I shall not be a saboteur. But give me a sign now and then and let some music flow from me, let what is within me be given expression, it longs so desperately for that.

—November 24, 1941, Monday, 5:30 p.m.

Cold, tummy ache, the house still in a great big mess.

I'm always asking myself nowadays, at moments when feelings of frustration threaten to overwhelm me: do you really mean it when you say you intend to take life seriously? It may well feel inspired to say at good moments, "I trust in God, I want to make something of my life, I accept all the suffering that will come my way." But do you seriously mean it, seeing that you wilt with every depression?

Still, lately I have not let myself wilt. I am trying hard to live on a more even keel, to lessen the swing between the ups and the downs. To mobilize all my strength, keep it mobilized, and yet to have dreams. One ought to be able to combine all these. In the past I wasted so many days just because of frustration. And spoiled myself too. Indulged myself reading books stretched out on divans and having lots of sleep and dreams. Until the moment arrived when I was full of energy again and ready for anything.

But if the moments when I feel that something inside me is trying hard to grow and when I resolve to use my time fruitfully are to be taken seriously and not considered as mere stray impulses, then I must carry on living and working even when I am feeling less inspired and more down-hearted, no matter how pointless it may seem at the time. Otherwise those moments of inspiration will be mere islands. One moment of true inspiration has to be able to shine out and give you strength for a long time. You are still asking for too much if you expect to live on the peaks and if you feel you're being short-changed whenever life is a bit dull and ordinary or just seems difficult. In the past, every time I felt the worse for wear and depressed from that monthly stomach ache, I thought I was being given carte blanche to do absolutely nothing, to let myself go and just wait until I felt like starting again. Don't get me wrong, you don't always have to live at such an intense level, indeed that might well be wrong for you, but you could try to give yourself a little push now and then, make a deliberate decision to follow a certain path, and try to stop letting yourself down each time. But things really have been a great deal better of late.

—December 2, 1941, Tuesday morning,
9:30 a.m. in the bathroom

I'm disgracefully disorganized. Perhaps that's the reason why I've been getting the feeling lately that I'm not doing enough, and at other times that my schedule is too full as it is and there's no room for more.

But it doesn't have to be like that at all, as well you know. My dear girl, what a complete washout you are. True, at the moment you feel awful and physically well below par, but that's no reason for chucking it all in. There's nothing clever about working, etc., at those times when you're feeling fit and well. It is precisely on days like these, on your off days, that you have to show what you are made of. Don't feel sorry for yourself. If you truly want to rise above the mediocre, then you're going to have to live differently.

Inner hygiene and organization. Not idling and frittering so much of your time away.

—December 4, Thursday morning, 9:00 a.m.

Han walks hurriedly through the room, sees me scribbling away here by the stove and asks with irony, "Are you thinking thoughts again? Are you expressing your feelings about the washing-up in more exalted form?" And I can't help thinking that he doesn't know what to make of it! The darling.

The last tin of apple syrup was finished at breakfast. But still two cups of tea, even though not unadulterated, and that after a good 1 year and a half of war. I shall start with a bit of grammar, go over that Bordewijk translation again and prepare Hetty's lesson. You dwell deep within me, God. I love this life. Han is meanwhile telling me for the 5 x 365th time how to strip a bed properly, and then he suddenly adds, "But don't let me disturb your more exalted thoughts." It is half past nine in the morning, the blackout curtains have already been pulled back but lots of lights are still on, the morning still looks somewhat dingy on the other side of the windows. Outside the house the broad frozen steppes will be stretching out again. And now get on with it, damn it.

—January 12, 1942, Monday morning, 9:00 a.m., by the little stove

SIMPLICITY OF SPEECH AND LIFESTYLE

Frugality of speech and simplicity of lifestyle are ways of focusing on the life of the spirit, inner truth, and the interior life. The monastic practices of silence and solitude form a blank canvas, as it were, against which words are spoken and one's own activities gauged. They strip the person of exterior embellishments and the unnecessary to allow the simple inner beauty to shine forth. Etty values simplicity of speech. As an aspiring writer, she is especially drawn to poets because they have developed the gift of conveying life's essentials or the soul of things by an economy of words. The German word for poetry is Dichtung, which literally translated means "compression." Uncertain about her writing talents, she repeatedly struggles with finding just the right words to express her insights. She is also aware of excesses in her life, especially in regard to books and her habit of reading voraciously. When Spier's two small rental rooms become too cramped to accommodate both his practice and living quarters, Etty volunteers to house his extensive library in her own room at Wegerif's. Having "1100 books" around her proves an ever-present temptation for gluttony and excess. Etty also recognizes that reveling in the experiences of physical pleasure, casual conversation, and entertainment activities seem unnecessary diversions and distract her from coming to rest in her center and allowing for communion with God. As far as living conditions were concerned, the war years (1939–45) had created an environment of dearth and scarcity of goods and food for people which by necessity imposed on them a lifestyle of simplicity.

As an assistant to Spier, Etty met with clients on her own, listening to them and conducting interviews and sessions. One of the clients was Liesl Levie,[11] mother of two young daughters, Miriam and Renate, and wife of Werner, an opera director. In Germany, "Every last thing of theirs had been ransacked, stolen, or burned" and they had fled to the Netherlands.

What shall I do this evening with that helpless little child-woman (she sometimes gives that impression)? She seems to

---

11. Liesl Levie would also become one of the members of the Spier circle.

expect something of me. I think I shall simply read her Jung's *The Meaning of Psychology for Modern Man*. And make certain that evenings with her do not degenerate into casual visits but that something positive results from them for both of us. In the past I was often so unthinking and casual in my dealings with my fellow men — you met and sometimes things went well; a spark might be suddenly struck and you would hang around a little bit longer. I shall not be able to do that any more now. Because there is now so palpable, so vital, so moving and deep a source within me and because I am constantly gaining greater clarity and precision, I no longer take any pleasure in muddled or random human relationships.

— January 14, 1942, Wednesday, 11:30 a.m.

To be very unobtrusive, and very insignificant, always striving for more simplicity. Yes, to become simple and live simply, not only within yourself but also in your everyday dealings. Don't make ripples around you, don't try so hard to be interesting, keep your distance, be honest, fight the desire to be thought fascinating by the outside world. Instead, reach for true simplicity in your inner life and in your surroundings. Yes, to be genuinely modest and simple, to wait, to be open, to allow growth and also work. Yes, work. It doesn't matter at what. I still haven't found solid ground under my feet, but whether it's Russian essays or reading Dostoevsky and Jung or having a talk, all of these can be work. And have confidence that it will all come together, and everything will turn out all right in the end. That confidence is something I've had for a long time. Works and deeds that mesh and fit together, and no empty spaces between them and a lot of steadfast and constant work. And being very very modest.   — April 1, 1942, Wednesday, early afternoon

Something else: at times I think that I will be able to write one day, to describe things, but then I suddenly grow tired and say

to myself, "Why all these words?" I want every word I write
to be born, truly born, none to be artificial, every one to be
essential. For otherwise there is no point to it at all. And that
is why I shall never be able to make a living by writing, why I
must always have a job to earn my keep. Every word born of
an inner necessity, writing must never be anything else.

                    — April 22, 1942, Wednesday, 11:00 p.m.

I shall have to give up chirology altogether and use the extra
time for my Russian studies. I must not split myself up between
things that are not essential for me. And I must have the
courage to tell him so. Last night, for instance, I stayed with
Aleida Schot[12] for a least an hour too long, I don't know why,
probably because I felt she would take it amiss if I left. If I were
really serious about life, that sort of thing would not happen. I
split myself up and dole myself out to things that are not necessary, neither for me nor for others, and always because of that
dependent feeling that I might hurt him and others, which is
no doubt a front for my fear that others might think less of
me. When all is said and done, that too is being dependent on
others, on the opinion others have of me, which is really their
business and not mine.   — June 4, 1942, Tuesday, 10:45 p.m.

Looked at Japanese prints with Glassner[13] this afternoon. That's
how I want to write. With that much space round a few words.
I hate wordiness. The only words I want to write are those naturally woven into one great silence, not those that merely serve
to drown out the silence and to pull it apart. They should simply emphasize the silence. Just like that print with the sprig of
blossom in the lower corner. A few delicate brush strokes —
but with what attention to the smallest detail — and around it

---

12. See p. 44, n. 8.
13. See p. 141, n. 21.

space, not empty but inspired. The few great things that matter in life can be said in a few words. I hate the accumulation of words. If I should ever write — but what? — I would like to brush in a few words against a wordless background. To describe the silence and the stillness and to inspire them. What matters is the right relationship between words and wordlessness, the wordlessness in which much more happens than in all the words one can string together.

— June 5, 1942, Friday evening, 7:30 p.m.

I should like to write a whole book about a pebble and about a purple pansy. I could live with nothing but a pebble for a long time and still feel that I was living in God's great world of nature. I really did not discover that pebble until the afternoon on the roof in the sun. It came straight from the Days of Creation, and my amazement at my sudden discovery of so many eternities in just one small pebble has refused to die down to this day....

Later when the war is over and we are again free to go where we want, I don't think I shall be spending much more time on light entertainment than I do now — I no longer feel I am missing out on life when I don't experience everything the entertainment world has to offer.

Good night.   — June 25, 1942, Thursday

If we have to share a prison cell with several others, isn't it our duty to keep our bodies and souls clean and fresh?

I find it curious and am less and less able to understand how some people can go on slogging away at extracting the maximum pleasure over and over again from their own and from each other's bodies. In a moment of candor a few days ago I told him, "Once upon a time I used to leap about in bed with a man for nights on end, but these days it does occur to me at times that it's really a sin and a waste to spend so much time and energy on one's own physical pleasure."

> — June 27, 1942, Saturday morning, 8:30 a.m.

Most people carry stereotyped ideas about life in their heads. We have to rid ourselves of all preconceptions, of all slogans, of all sense of security, find the courage to let go of everything, every standard, every conventional bulwark. Only then will life become infinitely rich and overflowing, even in the suffering it deals out to us.

I would so much like to read everything of Rilke's before the time comes when I won't perhaps be able to lay my hands on books for a long time. I feel very much at one with a small group of people I met by chance at Werner and Liesl's. All are being deported next week to work in Germany under police guard. Tonight I dreamed that I had to pack my case. I tossed and turned, fretting about what shoes to take — all of them hurt my feet. And how was I to pack all my underwear and food for three days and blankets into one suitcase or rucksack? And I had to find room somewhere for the Bible. And if possible for Rilke's *Book of Hours* and *Letters to a Young Poet*. And I very much wanted to take along my two small Russian dictionaries and *The Idiot* so as to keep up the language.

> — July 7, 1942, Tuesday afternoon

We must speak about the ultimate and most serious things in life only when the words well up inside us as simply and as naturally as water from a spring.

And if God does not help me to go on, then I shall have to help God.   — July 11, 1942, Saturday morning, 11 a.m.

I have a feeling that I must be economical with every word I utter. That I ought only to speak the most essential words. As if I had to store up inside everything that is dear and precious to me here, the better to carry a whole inalienable world away with me. Say only what is absolutely essential and for the rest become more and more concentrated in yourself.

Now that we are almost being ground down by the wheels of our times, times that may perhaps be called great one day, what matters is to raise God's banner high above the thousand fears and oppressions and despondencies of everyday life.

— July 27, 1942, Monday, 10:30 p.m.

But I still suffer from the same old complaint. I cannot stop searching for the great redeeming formula. For the one word that sums up everything within me, the overflowing and rich sense of life. "Why did You not make me a poet, oh God? But perhaps you did, and so I shall wait patiently until the words have grown inside me, the words that proclaim how good and beautiful it is to live in Your world, oh God, despite everything we humans do to one another."

The thinking heart of the barracks.

— September 15, 1942, Tuesday morning, 10:30 a.m.

HUMILITY IN CONFESSING ONE'S FAULTS

Practicing humility means recognizing one's faults and admitting them to oneself and before God. The goal is correcting these faults and doing better next time. Humility involves becoming aware of behavior and thoughts that prevent one from being one's true self, the person God created. Such awareness is painful, though it cannot be forced since it is a moment of grace. One of Etty's mottos is that "Grace during its rare appearances must be welcomed with a good/skilled/polished technique." Her technique is to chronicle her flaws and false ambitions in order to shed them and thus become more fully herself. To that end, her diary serves as an instrument and tool of confession, a silent confessor and a mirror to her soul: it receives her unflinchingly honest observations about her obsessions and attachments, as well as pronouncing in the firm voice of what could be a monastic superior or spiritual guide the admonitions, counsel, and affirmations she herself gives. Both frank in her admittance of guilt and gentle in receiving corrective remarks from herself, Etty begins to examine a whole host of flaws that, to her, are cluttering up the landscape of her soul and are causing her distress, anxiety, and confusion. She begins her examination of self shortly after meeting Spier and, probably at his suggestion, practices it almost daily by either making journal entries or reviewing mentally her responses to the world around her and others. On February 3, 1942, the day of her spiritual birthday on which she celebrates being "one year old" with her friends and Spier, Etty also submits to Spier a written report of an "annual confession." Probably part of Spier's therapeutic methods, the report was hand-written by Etty "in copperplate with blood and tears on fifteen sheets of notepaper": mistakes and flaws are now firmly etched into her awareness. Awareness of one's faults is an invitation to practice forgiveness toward one's self and increases compassion for others and their faults.

My protracted headaches: so much masochism; my abundant compassion: so much self-gratification. Compassion can be creative, but it can also be greedy. Objectivity is better than swooning in great emotions. For example, clinging to one's parents: one has to see them as people with a destiny of their own.

The desire to prolong ecstatic moments is misplaced. It's understandable, of course: you long for an hour's moving spiritual or "soulful" experience, even if it is followed by the inevitable jolt as you come down to earth again. Such jolts used to annoy me. I would be overcome with fatigue and pine for more of those exalted moments.

Call it by its proper name: ambition. What I put down on paper must be perfect right away; I don't like putting in the daily grind. And I'm not really sure of my own talent; it doesn't really feel like an organic part of me. In near-ecstatic moments I think myself capable of God knows what, only to sink back again into the deepest pit of uncertainty. That happens because I fail to work each day at what I believe is my real talent: writing. Theoretically I have known that for a long time; a few years ago I scribbled on a scrap of paper, "Grace during its rare appearances must be welcomed with a good/skilled/polished technique." But that was something that leaped out of my brain and still hasn't been translated into flesh and blood. Has a new phase of my life really begun? But the question mark is wrong. A new phase *shall* begin! Battle has been joined. "Battle" isn't right either, since at this moment I feel so good and harmonious, so utterly whole, or rather: my awareness is growing apace and everything that was locked up in my head until now in the shape of precisely worked-out formulae is about to flow into my heart. But my exaggerated self-consciousness will have to go first — I still enjoy this in-between state too much. Everything will have to become more straightforward, until in the end I shall, perhaps, finish up as an adult, capable of helping other souls who are in trouble, and of creating some sort of clarity through my work for others, for that's what it's really all about.
— March 12, 1941, Wednesday, 9:00 p.m.

No more feeble excuses now, get on with it, my girl; you've got the reins in your hands so don't let go of them. You never get anything for nothing, not for a single minute. But you are back on the straight and narrow now. That tidied-up kitchen is a reflection of your tidied-up mind.

Last Sunday I said to Pa Han, "Just go downstairs and have a look at the clean kitchen. It's an impression, a photograph, of my mental state." And only yesterday, before I went off to the

music, it was in an appalling mess. But this morning the first
job I did was the saucepans, and then the work surfaces, and as
soon as the shambles had been cleared away I could feel myself
calming down. And then the exercises, and now I'm back at my
desk, not yet completely filled with peace and space, but I shall
probably regain it in the course of the day.

—March 24, 1941, Monday morning, 9:30 a.m.

If I were a woman of true worth and greatness I would break
off all physical contact with him; it really does nothing but
upset me deeply. But I can't bring myself to renounce all the
possibilities that might then fall by the wayside. I think I am
also afraid that I might bruise his manliness. Still, our friendship would no doubt rise to a much higher level, and he would
presumably be grateful to me in the end if I helped him to stay
faithful to one woman. But I happen to be a particularly petty
and greedy person. Now and again I want to be back in his
arms, but then I end up unhappy all over again. There is probably a bit of childish vanity about it all as well. Something like:
here are all these girls and women who are mad about him,
yet I, who have known him for the shortest time of all, am the
only one with whom he is intimate. If that is truly what goes
on inside me, then it's absolutely sickening. Really I am running the risk of ruining our friendship for the sake of physical
pleasure. For of course, because of my not being able to give
myself completely physically just as I am — since deep, deep
down I don't really want to — I now and then resort to arti-
fice, to little erotic tricks and ruses which, of course, do not
come naturally to me and therefore find no echo in me, and it
is that which keeps making me feel so lonely. And because I am
not being completely natural, I become uncertain, am afraid to
disappoint him or to short-change him and, as a result, I cease
being frank with him and don't go to him with the same plea-

sure as I used to because I keep wondering beforehand, what is going to happen this time? That's probably the explanation of my fatigue, too.   — May 8, 1941, Friday, 8:00 p.m.

That spring fever has really been getting me down these last few days. And what infuriates me and makes me so resentful in the circumstances is that he goes on staying the same and is then guileless enough to say, "How nice to find a girl like you living her life as you do, giving everything a spiritual dimension."

Every so often I say to myself, I shan't be able to bear it much longer, I am getting desperate, I can't go on. And then, again, be patient. Bear the desire within you and allow it to grow. And stop all this childishness: feeling infuriated, provoked, and wronged by anyone who does not respond to your longings.

       — March 1, 1942, Sunday night, 8:30 p.m.

During the Beethoven, I silently begged forgiveness of Dicky's[14] listening profile with the childish mouth and the downturned eyelashes. I stroked her small snub nose with my little finger, and suddenly she was beaming at me with her small white teeth. I begged forgiveness for all the petty jealousies and irritations I sometimes feel toward her. She knows nothing about those irritations nor about my begging for forgiveness, but that's really none of her business. Yet something is sure to change in the atmosphere between us. It is only right and proper that one should be able to work on one's inner self for the purpose of improving human intercourse (how nauseatingly I keep putting things!), and that this is the only place where one can start, with oneself, in oneself. I can see no other way, and that way is becoming clearer and clearer to me.

       — March 16, 1942, Monday morning

---

14. Dicky de Jonge was part of the Spier circle and a renter at the Nethe house, where Spier also rented.

I had not prayed for a long time with so much concentration and so fervently as I did for those five minutes in the bathroom this morning. It seems I am entering a new phase of steadily increasing inner concentration. And that always happens as a reaction to the sudden realization of how close I had come once again to losing myself in endless abstractions. In that short prayer I also asked, "And please don't let me be vain." What I meant was this: more and more people are coming to bare their innermost thoughts to me and bring me their problems, and among them are interesting and worthy people, and I must make sure that my vanity isn't flattered because these people are drawn to me. In one way or another I must keep things on an impersonal level, create the right distance over and over again, and make it clear that what is involved are human problems, the clarification of difficulties and conflicts that happen by pure chance to have ended up in such and such a person. Then we can put our heads together to deal with the problems, carefully and lovingly — instead of forging too close a personal bond and thus reinforcing others in the wrong way. I especially have to guard against creating too great a personal bond with so young and passionate a girl as Hetty.

I said to S. recently, "She is so lovely to look at, with that young, passionate little face. A beautiful young girl like that inspires me much more than a plain one." To which, of course, S. retorted, "Yes, but that mustn't be the most important thing, or even the starting point." He himself has reached the point when he can help even the most unattractive people, even those he does not much care for personally, with as much devotion and love as those who are close to him. And that is how it ought to be.

I don't have to be afraid of being vain, it isn't really in me, but I must be true to myself all the time.

— March 23, 1942, Monday morning, 9:00 a.m.

My God, what a character! Just look at her jumping about on that divan! She must be a Russian. We don't do that sort of thing in Holland, do we? *An enfant terrible.*

I am still assailed far too much by words like these. I prayed early this morning, "Lord, free me from all these petty vanities. They take up too much of my inner life, and I know only too well that other things matter much more than being thought nice and charming by one's fellows." What I mean is, that sort of thing mustn't take up too much of your time and imagination. For then you get carried away with: "What a nice person I am, what fun I am, how much everyone must like me."

In the past I used to play the fool almost despite myself; and felt terribly unhappy doing it. Now I am sometimes madly exuberant just out of a surplus of energy, particularly on those days when I am most serious and concentrated inside. Then some hidden sort of childish elation bubbles out of me, sometimes bordering on silliness. That's all right. But if it becomes obvious that others are applauding such behavior, then it's time to make sure it isn't going to one's head or tickling one's vanity, for if that is allowed, one's focus will once again be shifted from the inner life toward the outer. As it is, I have been living a life of pleasure these past few days, and it is on just such days that I must be even more collected and peaceful inside, for if I am not then everything gets dissipated in vanity and play-acting.

Tonight from six o'clock onwards the dress rehearsal of the *Czardas Princess,*[15] tomorrow night with S. to the première of said Princess, after first dining with S. at Geiger's. On Sunday, Adri's birthday party at the Krijns,[16] in the afternoon some

---

15. Operetta by the Hungarian composer Emmerich Kalman (1882–1953); the production was the most grand-scale one of the Jewish Cabaret Ensemble of Amsterdam and was performed thirty times between April 18, 1942 and May 13, 1942. To keep as many people as possible from deportation, the number of actors and technicians was made as large as possible.

16. Adri Holm, a member of the Spier circle, had her birthday party at the house of Spier's sister and brother-in-law, Alice and Leo Krijn.

music, in the evening a meal and a little dancing, etc. Next Saturday it will be S.'s birthday. Twelve of us will be having a meal at Geiger's, then on to the Levies. Sunday morning some music here and perhaps supper at the Glassners'. All these are festive occasions, but they must not be blown up out of proportion. I must not start thinking already about what sort of dress I shall wear for the Levies, how seductively I shall dance, and how much I'll be appreciated by everyone.

Yesterday I was struck by this sentence in Rilke:

"...a time must come when I am alone with my experience, belonging to it, reshaping it: for even now, all that is untransformed oppresses and confuses me...."[17]

Yes: to belong to one's experience. And to transform it. That is my great yearning as well. We must carry our experience within us, place it at the center of a quiet space within us and hearken to it there. That is something you cannot do if you pay too much heed to the enthusiasms assailing your poor self from without. To be alone. Stillness. No matter how much of a bustling crowd there is about you. No vanity!

—April 17, 1942, Friday morning, 9:00 a.m.

I remembered how, last week in that wretched little ice cream parlor, crammed full of yellow stars, I said to Liesl, "If only we don't become too smug, we have to watch out for that, we who have discovered our inner reality."

Always attuning oneself to others, remembering how difficult one's own road to this inner reality has been and how one has to rediscover it over and over again.

In the middle of a conversation last night, when my all too great reticence was mentioned and I said that I could only speak about those things in myself that are "rounded off," he suddenly turned on me, saying this was a misconception on my

_____

17. Rilke, *Letters 1902–1906*.

part. That one is never rounded off, and that one must have the courage to show how one is developing, even if one is not yet "rounded off." I then said that sometimes I felt it as a personal shortcoming, when I compared my temperament, spontaneity, quick grasp of things, and briskness in seeing to externals with my sluggish inner process. That whenever I speak about myself I have the feeling that I am splitting myself up, and then I always feel torn into pieces and very sad. Yet I have a need to explain myself to others, and it probably sounds very pretentious when I say that I feel impelled to explain my inner processes to all mankind. Not to some individual in a private conversation but to all mankind, yes, all of them, in the form of some masterpiece or other. It is nonsense of course, sitting at my desk and making a fool of myself because I can't find the right words, but sometimes I feel as if everything I experience deep down is not just for me, that I have no right to keep it to myself, that I must account for it. (S. said rightly tonight that my reticence may well reflect my strong possessiveness.)

As if in this tiny slice of human history I were one of the many receiving sets which have to transmit messages. But I don't yet know just what these messages are.

If I weren't too tired to take stock of today, I would express my dissatisfaction with the way I spoke to Hetty about the theater. She probably didn't even notice, but it bothers me. For there was a touch of: "I am a woman utterly at ease in those circles, completely at home with it all." And some vague generalities that did nothing for anybody. [*Then S. made some*] lucid remarks. While I dished up vaguely sensational stories, like a real "insider," and at the same time spoke very arrogantly and with distaste about this group of people,[18] disparaging them. That sort of thing gives me an immediate hangover. When one

---

18. Referring to actors.

cannot stand by every word one says, one would do far better not to say anything at all. You humbug, trying to impress
others, you ought to be ashamed of yourself!

— June 4, 1942, Thursday, about midnight, in the bathroom

One must live with oneself as if one lived with a whole nation
of people. And in oneself one then comes to recognize all the
good and bad qualities of mankind. And if one wants to forgive
others, one must first learn to forgive one's own bad qualities.

That is probably the hardest thing a person can learn, as I
so often find in others (in myself as well in the past, but no
longer): to forgive one's own mistakes and lapses. Which means
accepting above all, and magnanimously, that one does make
mistakes and does have lapses.

— September 22, 1942, Thursday

3

Self and World as One

SADNESS, SUFFERING, AND PATIENCE

The experience of sadness, gloom, and emotional turmoil is an intricate part of the human condition. Often these states are classified or diagnosed as cases of depression for which medication and treatment are quickly sought and prescribed. However, experiencing and bearing periods of pain and suffering can have a redemptive and healing effect. In the early monastic tradition of the East, the state of gloom and depression was called the "noon-day demon," linking this state with a spiritual condition rather than a physical one, such as mental illness. Given that members of her own family had been diagnosed with mental illness by psychiatrists, Etty is concerned that her own protracted periods of sadness and gloom may be indicators that she, too, is "mad." With Spier's help, she begins to bear these periods of suffering, chronicling in her diary the times they occurred and what had preceded them, and tracing their possible causes to attitudes and expectations of which she had been previously unaware. Once she has identified the emotional attitudes that could have triggered her sadness or internal unease, she sets to work at changing them. She says that the "ego with its desires, which merely serve to satisfy that highly restricted ego, must be eradicated and extinguished." In her case, the root causes of unease and gloom are pride, or vanity, ambition, and possessiveness. Thus, the pain and suffering she experiences become to her a school of patience with redemptive power, resulting in a repeated new "birth," and are helping her to emotionally mature in the process. In bearing the temporary discomfort and allowing for the reconciliation of contending inner forces to occur gradually, often in conjunction with prayer, she learns patience, a virtue she hopes to help others cultivate also as they face suffering and pain, caused by their own attitudes or by a world that inflicts it on them.

For a moment yesterday I thought I couldn't go on living, that I needed help. Life and suffering had lost their meaning for me; I felt I was about to collapse under a tremendous weight. But once again I put up a fight and now I can face it all, stronger than before. I have tried to look that "suffering" of mankind fairly and squarely in the face. I have fought it out, or rather something in me has fought it out, and suddenly there were answers to many desperate questions, and the sense of emptiness made way for the feeling that there was order and meaning after all, and I could get on with my life. All was smooth going again after a short but violent battle from which I emerged just a fraction more mature.

I said that I confronted the "Suffering of Mankind" (I still shudder when it comes to big words), but that was not really what it was. Rather I feel like a small battlefield, in which the problems, or some of the problems, of our time are being fought out. All one can hope to do is to keep oneself humbly available, to allow oneself to be a battlefield. After all, the problems must be accommodated, have somewhere to struggle and come to rest, and we, poor little humans, must put our inner space at their service and not run away. In that respect, I am probably very hospitable; mine is often an exceedingly bloody battlefield, and dreadful fatigue and splitting headaches are the toll I have to pay. Still, now I am myself once again Etty Hillesum, an industrious student in a friendly room with books and a vase of oxeye daisies. I am flowing again in my own narrow riverbed, and my desperate involvement with "Mankind," "World History," and "Suffering" has subsided. And that's as it should be; otherwise one might go mad. One ought not to lose oneself forever in the great questions, one cannot always be a battlefield, one must, time and again, feel one's small boundaries within which one goes on living one's own small life conscientiously and consciously, forever ripened and deepened by one's experiences during the almost "impersonal" moments of contact with mankind as a whole. Later, I shall probably be able to put it better or allow a character in a short story or a novel to say these things, but that will only be very much later.

— June 15, 1941, Sunday, noon

I feel as if I had written nothing in this exercise book for months, as if I had become untrue to myself in some way and had allowed things to slide. It's been lack of time and also a feeling that there was no need. For a few weeks I thought I was living a very secure and regular life, but in retrospect it seems to have been otherwise. Suddenly I have the feeling that living a balanced life means nothing more than walking a tightrope above the abyss. I really must work much more regularly "on myself," keep a careful watch on myself, but that is where the real trouble starts. I have the feeling now that I am a psychological laboratory in which a large number of processes are taking place, enough for dozens of people. It would take all my time to commit all of these processes to paper. Of course I could always force myself to write for, say, half an hour every morning. But things generally refuse to crystallize from my chaotic state, so that all I'm able to write about is a lot of trivial, irrelevant details. Even so, I'm sure that it's important for me to keep in close contact with myself and to give an account of myself. It is important, after all, for me to know how I manage to get over the various kinds of depression I have every time, so that I may perhaps show the way to others in the future.

— September 24, 1941, Wednesday morning

On the one hand, I feel I ought to make an academic study of literature, writing essays about it, and on the other hand, I am bubbling with all the inner sources that make me want to write and create original work. And at the same time I keep wondering whether there is anything at all inside me, and if I am not overrating myself. But what does it really matter, little one? Why must I be able to *do* anything? Why do I have to prove myself to the outside world? Surely it is enough that a bit of everything should exist within me. You need to be patient and honest and without ambition, not want to *be* anything.

— September 29, 1941, Monday morning, 10:00 a.m.

While cataloguing S.'s books, I unexpectedly came across Rilke's *Book of Hours*.

Paradoxical though it may sound: S. heals people by teaching them how to suffer and accept.

— December 13, 1941, Saturday, 2:00 p.m.

Suddenly my neck bowed down over this dark surface, under the weight of my thoughts. How will I ever be able to write it all down?

I thought this yesterday: there is a big difference between the sensual enjoyment of going in search of suffering, and accepting it as it comes. The first is an unhealthy masochism; the second is a healthy acceptance of life. Nor need we go in search of "suffering," but whenever it thrusts itself upon us we must not avoid it. And it thrusts itself upon us at every step, but life is beautiful for all that. We suffer most by playing hide and seek with suffering and calling curses down upon it. Of course that's not quite what I have been thinking, but let me at least have the courage to pen a few faltering words. Who knows but that they may not later turn into so many imperfect hat stands on which I can then hang some more mature thoughts.

And a bit later during the day I came across this in Suarès: "Pain is not the site of our longing but the site of our certainty. ...I do not claim that we must look upon pain as perfection. Indeed, we must do all we can to rid ourselves of it. But we must be acquainted with pain. Real man is neither master of his pain, nor a fugitive from it, nor its slave: he must be pain's redeemer."[1]

—December 15, 1941, Monday morning, 9:30 a.m.

This, too, is one of my latest achievements: the realization that every moment gives birth to a new moment, full of fresh potential, and sometimes like an unexpected present. And that one must not cling to moments of malaise and prolong them needlessly, because in so doing one may prevent the birth of a richer moment. Life courses through one as a constant current in a great series of moments, each having its own place in the day. Come on now, can't you do better than that? I can't help it, truly, I still can't put it into words. Hush now, be patient. And if you can't say it, then someone else will do it for you, Rilke or Beethoven, for instance.

—December 31, 1941, Wednesday, 10 a.m.

I remember a walk along an Amsterdam canal, one dreamlike summer night, long, long ago. I had visions then of ruined cities. I saw old cities vanish and new cities arise, and I thought to myself: even if the whole of this world is bombed to bits, we

---

1. Quoted from the Dostoevsky biography, *Dostojewski*, by André Suarès (1868–1948), who had also written biographies of Blaise Pascal and Henrik Ibsen.

shall build a new world, and that one too will pass, and still life will be beautiful, always beautiful. It was just a vision. Cities tumbling into the abyss and new ones rising up, and so on through the ages, and life, which is so beautiful.

Does that mean I am never sad, that I never rebel, always acquiesce, and love life no matter what the circumstances? No, far from it. I believe that I know and share the many sorrows and sad circumstances that a human being experiences, but I do not cling to them, I do not prolong such moments of agony. They pass through me, like life itself; as a broad, eternal stream, they become part of that stream, and life continues. And as a result all my strength is preserved, does not become tagged onto futile sorrow or rebelliousness.

And finally: ought we not, from time to time, open ourselves up to cosmic sadness? One day I shall surely be able to say to Ilse Blumenthal,[2] "Yes, life is beautiful, and I value it anew at the end of every day, even though I know that the sons of mothers, and you are one such mother, are being murdered in concentration camps. And you must be able to bear your sorrow; even if it seems to crush you, you will be able to stand up again, for human beings are so strong, and your sorrow must become an integral part of yourself; part of your body and your soul. You mustn't run away from it, but bear it like an adult. Do not relieve your feelings through hatred, do not seek to be avenged on all German mothers, for they, too, sorrow at this very moment for their slain and murdered sons. Give your sorrow all the space and shelter in yourself that is its due, for if

2. Ilse Blumenthal-Weiss (1899–1987) was a journalist employed in Germany at the *Jewish Magazine* and a contributor to the *Annual of Jewish History and Literature;* she had fled to the Netherlands in 1937 and worked for a Dutch weekly magazine in Amsterdam, where she met Etty. They met again in 1943 in Westerbork. She survived the concentration camp and emigrated to the United States in 1947. In her early twenties, Blumenthal had wanted to be a poet (later publishing four volumes of poetry) and had corresponded with Rilke. Etty disagreed with Blumenthal's assessment of Rilke as "soft."

everyone bears his grief honestly and courageously, the sorrow that now fills the world will abate. But if you do not clear a decent shelter for your sorrow, and instead reserve most of the space inside you for hatred and thoughts of revenge — from which new sorrows will be born for others — then sorrow will never cease in this world and will multiply. And if you have given sorrow the space its gentle origins demand, then you may truly say: life is beautiful and so rich. So beautiful and so rich that it makes you want to believe in God."

> — March 28, 1942, Saturday morning, 10:00 a.m.

My patience still has to grow. I have already acquired enough, though, to wait for what is coming, to have trust in the fact that something is coming. I still don't know if I have the patience to walk by myself for hours through a lonely landscape, to live alone in a fishing village by the sea and to be content with my own thoughts. I still lack the patience to pass my time with flowers and to listen to music and to look at paintings and to read the Bible. I still have to learn all that, learn a whole life long. But I do believe that I am making a start. And every so often there comes that great patience, the ultimate source on which I can draw for any creative work I may do. But I'm sure that that patience is still being interrupted all the time by my restlessness. I must learn to gather up all the patience that is in me, gather together all the fragments of patience into one great patience. And perhaps, perhaps, much later — I may then be able to write. There is Käthe now. I must rush off and help her with the breakfast, nice, faithful, good old Käthe!

> — April 4, 1942, Saturday morning, 8:00 a.m.

For the fourth time, Etty copies out here the same passage from Rilke's Letters to a Young Poet; *the first time she does so is on February 16, 1942.*

I am copying it out once more, for the umpteenth time I must drum it firmly into my mind, over and over again:

"There is no measuring of time then, a year does not matter then and ten years are as nothing. Being an artist means not calculating and counting; coming to maturity like a tree which does not force its sap, which continues to stand confidently throughout the spring storms, never doubting that summer will come. It will. But it comes only to the patient, who behave as if eternity lay before them, so carefree, still, and spacious are they. Every day I keep learning it, learning it painfully, for which I am grateful: patience is all!"

—June 4, 1942, Thursday morning, 9:30 a.m.

One day I shall have to assimilate everything I know about life and people. At every turn recently, an appropriate Rilke sentence has demanded my attention. Just now I came across this one in a letter:

"More and more (and fortunately for me) I live the existence of the kernel in the fruit, which orders everything in itself and out of itself in the darkness of its workings. And more and more I see that living like that is my only way out; else I cannot transform the sourness about me into the sweetness I have ever owed the dear Lord."[3]   —June 10, 1942, Wednesday, nighttime
                                    while reading a really good novel

From time to time one should keep a tight rein on one's agitation, lest it rear up and like a bolting horse run riot through one's entire being; one's sadness, too, should be held in check, lest it rise like a river in flood to swamp all one's laboriously tilled fields. One should try to stop being so egocentric as to let every mood run its full course. One need not conceal one's disquiet and sadness; one should bear them and forbear them,

---

3. From Rilke, *Letters 1906–1907*.

but not surrender to them as unreservedly as if there were nothing else in the world. One should no longer consign one's best endeavors to sadness, but save them — ultimately that is the least one can do — for the community, to use a big word. And by community, I mean a pupil who comes to learn Russian from you, a fellow human being who comes to you with his problems, a poem that demands your attention in order to be understood.

In the past I considered it my right to succumb to every twinge of sadness; everything had to make way for it, and nothing was of any importance compared with the great huge grief that filled my entire being. That no longer happens, although things can still come quite closely to it sometimes.... No, sadness must not be allowed to gain such a hold over one. At least not any longer, not as one grows older. One has known and been through it all, but one can't keep going on like that, because in the long run that is nothing but egocentricity and dissipating your best endeavors....

I spoke to someone yesterday who had met Rilke a few times in the sanatorium at Valmont.[4] The words in her account that made the strongest impression on me were "a gloomy man but very friendly."

And isn't that how it should be? Not taking one's own gloominess, sadness, or what have you out on others by being unfriendly to them? When we suffer, surely we don't have to make others suffer with us? If only people would begin to realize that! It is a process of growing awareness, one that every person must learn for himself. But those who have already made a start with that process must give the first push to others who are still "unborn." Ultimately that must be my way of doing "social work." I am unsuited to any other method.
— June 11, 1942, Thursday, 9:00 a.m.

---

4. The sanatorium in Switzerland where Rilke died in December of 1926.

One must be able to bear things, bear them to the bitter end and at their full weight. Suddenly I wondered, isn't that the difference between the Russians and us Westerners? The Russian bears his burden to the end, buckles down under the full weight of his emotions and suffers to his very depths. We stop halfway and relieve ourselves with words, reflections, philosophies, theoretical treatises, and what have you. We stop in the middle of experiencing our emotions, can bear and endure them no further, and our brains come to our aid, rid us of our burden and build their theories on it. . . .

We deprive ourselves of the ultimate suffering and cast it off with words. The Russian bears it to the end, and unless he perishes as a result he grows ever stronger.

— June 28, 1942, Sunday morning, 9:00 a.m.

Suffering is not beneath human dignity. I mean: it is possible to suffer with dignity and without. I mean: most of us in the West don't understand the art of suffering and experience a thousand fears instead. We cease to be alive, being full of fear, bitterness, hatred, and despair. . . .

One must also have enough strength to suffer alone and not to burden others with one's fears and troubles. That is something we still have to learn; we shall have to teach it to one another, and if it can't be done gently then let it be done harshly. . . .

Am I blasé then? No. It is a question of living life from minute to minute and taking suffering into the bargain. And it is certainly no small bargain these days. But does it matter if it is the Inquisition that causes people to suffer in one century, and war and pogroms in another? To suffer senselessly, as the victims would put it? Suffering has always been with us — does it really matter in what form it comes? All that matters is how we bear it and how we fit it into our lives and yet continue to accept these. Am I merely an armchair theorist safely ensconced behind my desk, with my familiar books around me and the jasmine outside? Is it all theory, never tested in practice? I don't think so. I'm aching all over, and soon I shall be walking with S. to the other end of town and we shall see a whole lot of trams going by that could have carried us there much more quickly than our legs.[5] And before very long we will have to be registered; it seems to be the turn of Dutch people now, including girls. ("You must not leave," S. told me yesterday firmly; and Käthe pointed to her bottled strawberries and said, "I hope he'll still be there to enjoy these strawberries with us." Yes, all our conversations are now interlarded with such sentences.) Mischa had to walk to the station yesterday, and at home they are bound to end up butchering each other these long summer evenings after eight o'clock, and I think of Miriam's and Renate's[6] pale little faces, and of many, many worried people, and I know it all, everything, every moment, and I sometimes bow my head under the great burden that weighs down on me, but even as I bow my head I also feel the need, almost mechanically, to fold my hands. And so I can sit for hours and know everything and bear everything and grow stronger in the bearing of it, and at the same time feel sure that life is beautiful and worth living and meaningful. Despite everything.

— July 2, 1942, Thursday, 7:30 a.m.

ETHICS OF LOVE

The ability to love others springs from the ability to first love oneself. The love for self, one's soul, the place where God dwells deep within, comes from acknowledging one's own faults and weaknesses and forgiving oneself for them. Love of

---

5. At that time, Jews were required to wear a yellow star for self-identification and were no longer allowed to take trams.

6. The two Levie daughters.

neighbor begins with love of self and a tender and compassion-
ate care for the place and "image" of God within. Through the
study of scripture, Etty is introduced to this principle and begins
practicing it: she probes her lack of love for self, seeks to iden-
tify its reasons, and turns to prayer to have self-love restored in
her. Once restored, she is capable of sensing her love for others.
In time, she can see people's spiritual dimension and make-up.
She recognizes that many people lack awareness of their soul,
thus being troublesome, unloving, and hateful toward others.
Since they do not sufficiently love themselves, they do not and
cannot love others. Etty wants to help them, rather than accus-
ing and judging them for their lack of self-love. Moved by
compassion for their blindness, with which she can readily iden-
tify, she intentionally places herself in their company and makes
herself available as a giver of love and a teacher on God and the
soul. Her decision to work for the Jewish Council and her vol-
unteering at Camp Westerbork are partly motivated by a desire
to guide others into becoming more loving toward themselves:
she wants to be a healing presence, a dispenser of kindness, a
balm for all wounds.

Last night I felt that I must ask for forgiveness for all the ugly
and rebellious thoughts I have had about him these last few
days. I have gradually come to realize that on those days when
you are at odds with your neighbors, you are really at odds with
yourself. "Thou shalt love thy neighbor as thyself."[7] I know
that the fault is always mine, not his. Our two lives happen to
have quite different rhythms; one must allow other people the
freedom to be what they are. Trying to coerce others, of course,
is quite undemocratic, but only too human. It is psychology that
will probably pave the way to true freedom. We tend to forget
that not only must we gain inner freedom from one another,

---

7. In reference to Leviticus 19:18, also to Mark 12:31 and Matthew 22:39.

but we must also leave the other free and abandon any fixed concept we may have of him in our imagination. There is scope enough for the imagination as it is, without our having to use it to shackle the people we love....

I have recently been picking odd sentences from the Bible and endowing them with what for me is a new, meaningful, and experiential significance. God created man in His own image.[8] Love thy neighbor as thyself. Etcetera.

My relationship with my father is something I shall at long last have to tackle as well — with determination and love.

Mischa announced that Father would be arriving on Saturday evening. First reaction: Oh, my God. My freedom threatened. A nuisance. What am I to do with him? Instead of: How nice that this lovable man has managed to get away for a few days from his excitable spouse and his dull provincial town. How can I make things as pleasant as possible for him with my limited resources and means? Wretched, good-for-nothing, indolent worm that I am. Oh yes, the cap fits. Always think of yourself first, of your precious time — time you only use to pump more book-learning into your addled brain. "What shall it profit me if I have no love?"[9] Fine theories to make you feel comfortable and noble, but in practice you shrink from even the smallest act of love. No, what is needed here is not a small act of love. It is something fundamental and important and difficult. To love your parents deep inside. To forgive them for all the trouble they have given you by their very existence: by tying you down, by adding the burden of their own complicated lives to your own. I think I am writing a lot of nonsense. Well, no matter. Now I must make up Pa Han's bed, prepare the lesson for that girl Levi, etc. But the main item for this weekend's program: to love my father deeply and sincerely and to forgive

---

8. In reference to Genesis 1:27.
9. In reference to 1 Corinthians 13:1–3.

him for disturbing my pleasure-seeking life. When all is said and done I think a great deal of him, but in a rather complicated way: my love for him is forced, spasmodic, and so mixed with compassion that my heart almost breaks. Masochistic compassion. A love that leads to outbursts of sadness and pity, but not to simple acts of tenderness. Instead there is much effusiveness and a desire to please so violent that each day of one of his visits once cost me a whole tube of aspirins. But that was a long time ago. The last time things were much better. But still, there is always that hunted feeling as well as the related wish that he wouldn't always bring his troubles to me. And for that I must learn to forgive him this time. And also learn to think and genuinely mean: How nice that you have managed to get away. Well, that's a prayer for this morning.

— November 28, 1941, Friday morning, 8:45 a.m.

One should always be ready to meet one's fellow men constructively, and the more constructive one is, the better.

I am so grateful for this life. I feel I am growing, I am aware of my faults and my pettinesses each new day, but I also know my potential. And I have so much love; I love a few good friends, but that love is not a fence erected against others; my love is far-flung, all-embracing and broad enough to include very many of whom I am really not all that fond. It is now 10 o'clock. Han is sleeping upstairs again next to his somewhat melodramatic, pneumonia-stricken son, and I am creeping gratefully into my narrow, solitary bed. Curious, whenever I lie there stretched out on my back, I feel just as if I were clinging to Mother Earth herself, though I am actually lying on my soft mattress. But as I lie there like that, intense and outstretched and full of gratitude for everything, it is just as if I were at one with — well, with what? With the earth, with the sky, with God, with everything. And truly, it does feel as if I were clinging to the earth herself and not to a genuinely bourgeois, soft and decadent mattress. And now goodnight.

— February 22, 1942, Sunday evening, 9:00 p.m.

The night before, Spier had read to Etty on the telephone an extract from a letter sent to him by his fiancée, Hertha Levi; another letter of Hertha's had arrived in the morning.

And when I sat down in front of the stove after I came back yesterday afternoon,[10] feeling so sad, which was at first incomprehensible to me, and reread Leonie's letter, I reached for my Bible and opened it at 1 Corinthians 13 for the umpteenth time.

Yes.

"Though I speak with the tongues of men and of angels, and have not charity, I am become as sounding brass, or a tinkling cymbal.

"And though I have the gift of prophecy, and understand all mysteries, and all knowledge; and though I have all faith, so that I could remove mountains, and have not charity, I am nothing. . . .

"Charity suffereth long, and is kind; charity envieth not; charity vaunteth not itself, is not puffed up, doth not behave itself unseemly, seeketh not her own, is not easily provoked, thinketh no evil."

And when I read these words, I felt as if — yes, as if what? I cannot yet express it properly. They worked on me like a divining rod that touched the bottom of my heart, causing hidden sources to spring up suddenly within me. All at once I was down on my knees beside the little white table and all my released love coursed through me again, purged of desire, envy, spite, etc.   — February 25, 1942, Wednesday, 4:00 p.m.

---

10. Presumably from Spier's place.

After reflecting on Spier's worries for family members who had been arrested by the Nazis and concern for having failed to register both property and family capital:

We could be ordered at any moment to those barracks in Drenthe Province, and the greengrocers have signs in their shops saying, "No Jews." The average person has more than enough on his plate these days. But he still sees six patients a day and gives all he has to each one. He breaks them open and draws out the poison and delves down to the sources where God hides Himself away. And he works with such intensity that, in the end, the water of life begins to flow again in dried-up souls; each day the life stories pile up on his little table, almost every one ending with, "Please help me." And there he is ready and willing to help each one. Last night in my bathroom novel I read the following passage about a priest: "He was a mediator between God and men. Nothing worldly ever touched him. And that was why he understood the need of all who were still busy growing...."[11]

Are his energies so used up by the many who need him each day that he simply had to turn away from me? Etty, I loathe you. So selfish and so mean. Instead of supporting him with your love and caring, you fret like a spoiled child because he isn't paying enough attention to you. It is a petty woman indeed who wants all a man's attention and love for herself alone.

— June 13, 1942, Saturday morning

I needed a great many circuitous routes and thickets of words this gloomy, rainy morning to arrive at a simple, clear view of things. Among the far too many, yet essential, words of this morning I wrote something along these lines: one sometimes

---

11. Quoted from Von Urbanitzky, *Eine Frau erlebt die Welt* ("A Woman Experiences the World"), 1931.

tries to compensate for a temporary lack of inner resources by making demands on the outside world, with the quite unreasonable expectation that it will replenish those resources.

But I ought to have added this: at times when I have no love in me, or at least do not feel it alive in me, I try to compensate for it by demanding extra supplies of love from my nearest and dearest. I might just as well refrain from doing that, because even if they were to shower me with all their love I shouldn't know what to do with it, and I wouldn't even experience it as love because it finds no response in me. And that starts a process in which one becomes more and more demanding still. One could almost reduce it to a short algebraic formula: a shortage or lack of love within me makes me demand twice the helping of love from without. And even if they gave it to me, I couldn't know what to do with it.

However — and this is a new question — how does one temporarily run out of love? But that is a chapter all to itself, and perhaps it is much simpler than I think, but now I must prepare some little translation exercises for my bean man.[12]

— June 13, 1942, Saturday, at the end of the morning

Repeatedly Etty struggles with feeling unloved by Spier, hence feeling disillusioned with the relationship and, most of all, with herself and her ongoing mood swings. She blames her "deeply rooted preconceptions" of what a relationship should be and the "leftover from cheap romances: all or nothing."

After meditating beside the pearwood bookcase:[13]

You must never turn a person, no matter how beloved, into the object of your life. It is all a matter of ends and means. The

---

12. By "bean man" she means a green grocer who was one of her Russian students who supplied them with beans, among other things.

13. The bookcase was Spier's and had been moved to Etty's to hold his books.

aim is life itself in all its forms. And every person is a mediator between you and life. Life lends its gestures and contents
and forms to people, and from every person we learn about
life in a different form. We learn about people from life, the
more to learn about life, but then we have to let them go again
and return them to life, no matter how hard we may find that.
And those we love most are probably the ones from whom we
learn most about life. Or perhaps that's wrong. Doesn't our
love block our outlook on life? Yes, but only when it turns the
beloved into an end.

                    — June 15, 1942, Monday morning, 8:00 a.m.

The whole world is in me, and though I am tired and though
I am sad or afraid, the whole world is in me all the same; it
is always there and keeps growing. "World" is, of course, the
wrong term; it is much more than that. And I have taken in
something this past year that will never leave me again. But he
must remain in good health. And safe. They must not take him
away, they mustn't.[14] Because I should then have to summon all
my strength from every corner of my body and soul and concentrate it into one great, uninterrupted prayer for him. But please
let nothing happen to him, I wouldn't know how to carry on.
Just think of all the other people who no longer know how to
carry on with their lives and who, although alive, have already
done a lot of dying. One must not die while still alive; one has
to live one's life to the full and to the end. Even if something
were to happen to him? Yes, I would have to live on in his
spirit then, and pray for him, day and night. I feel so strange.
Everything that up till now has seemed so unreal is increasingly becoming a reality, an inner one so far. As if the whole
process of giving birth were taking place within. A process

---

14. Referring to the possibility of Spier's deportation to a prison camp for having
failed to register family capital.

of displacement. Outwardly everything remains the same. One cannot talk about that inner displacement because one does not yet have control over one's voice and because it would sound almost intolerably grandiloquent. One thing, though, is certain: we must help to increase the store of love in this world. Every bit of hate we add to the surfeit of hate there already is, renders this world more inhospitable and uninhabitable. When it comes to love I have so much, so very much, that it really counts for something, is no longer wanting. And now I really must go to bed.... —July 4, 1942, Sunday, 12:45 a.m. at night in Dicky's room [at the Nethe house, where Spier rented rooms]

Even if one's body aches, the spirit can continue to do its work, can it not? It can love and *hineinhorchen* — "hearken unto" — itself and unto others and unto what binds us to life. *Hinein-horchen* — I so wish I could find a Dutch equivalent for that German word. Truly, my life is one long hearkening unto my self and unto others, unto God. And if I say that I hearken, it is really God who hearkens inside me. The most essential and the deepest in me hearkening unto the most essential and deepest in the other. God to God.

"How great are the needs of Your creatures on this earth, O God. I thank You for letting so many people come to me with their inner needs. They sit there, talking quietly and quite unsuspectingly, and suddenly their need erupts in all its naked-ness. Then, there they are, bundles of human misery, desperate and unable to face life.

"And that's when my task begins. It is not enough simply to proclaim You, God, to commend You to the hearts of others. One must also clear the path toward You in them, God, and to do that one has to be a keen judge of the human soul. A trained psychologist. Ties to father and mother, youthful mem-ories, dreams, guilt feelings, inferiority complexes, and all the rest block the way. I embark on a slow voyage of exploration with everyone who comes to me. The stock of tools I need to pave the path towards You in others is still very limited. But some tools are there already, and I shall hone them, slowly and patiently. And I thank You for the great gift of being able to read people. Sometimes they seem to me like houses with open doors. I walk in and roam through passages and rooms, and every house is furnished a little differently, and yet they are all of them the same, and every one must be turned into a dwelling dedicated to You, O God. And I promise You, yes, I promise that I shall try to find a dwelling and a refuge for You in as many houses as possible. This really is a droll metaphor. I shall go along the path and try to find a dwelling for You. There are so many empty houses, and I shall prepare them all for You, the most honored lodger. Please forgive this poor metaphor."

— September 17, 1942, Thursday morning, 8:00 a.m.

"How can I thank You, oh God, for all the good You keep showering upon me. For all the friendship, for the many fruitful thoughts, for that great all-embracing love I feel within me and that I am able to apply at every step. Sometimes I almost believe that it is too much, and then I cannot tell how I shall ever do justice to it. But it is just as if, thanks to that great love, everything one does bears fruit. Perhaps I shall yet be able to put it into words."

— September 20, 1942, Sunday morning, 10:00 a.m.

Verbalize, vocalize, visualize.

Many people are still hieroglyphics to me, but gradually I am learning to decipher them. It is the best I can do: to read life from people.

In Westerbork it was as if I stood before the bare palisade of life. Life's innermost framework, stripped of all outer trappings. "Thank You, God, for teaching me to read better and better...." "After this war, two torrents will be unleashed on

the world: a torrent of loving-kindness and a torrent of hatred."
And then I knew: I should take the field against hatred.

— September 20, 1942, Sunday night

Etty is telling the writer Klaas Smelik (who at her request received Etty's diaries and letters after her death) about a colleague of hers at the Jewish Council who had served at Westerbork; the man, a capable and renowned lawyer, was noted for his cruel and heartless treatment of people, including fellow Jews.

That's how it was, Klaas, in fact: he was full of hatred towards those you could call our executioners, but what an excellent executioner and prosecutor of defenseless people he himself would have made. And yet I felt so sorry for him. Can you understand any of this? There was never any real contact between him and others, and he would give such covert, hungry looks whenever other people were friendly to each other. (I could always see him do it, for we lived a life without walls there.) Later I heard a few things about him from a colleague who had known him for years. During the German invasion he jumped into the street from a third-floor window but failed to kill himself. Later he threw himself under a car, but again to no avail. He then spent a few months in a mental institution. It was fear, just fear. He was such a brilliant and sharp-witted lawyer, and in debates with professors and other academics he always had the last word. But at the critical moment he jumped out of a window with fear. I also learned that his wife had had to walk on tiptoe in the house because he could not bear the slightest noise and that he used to storm at his terrified children. I felt such deep, deep pity for him. What sort of life was that? In the end he hanged himself.

Klaas, all I really wanted to say is this: we have so much work to do on ourselves that we shouldn't even be thinking of hating our so-called enemies. We are hurtful enough to one another as it is. And I don't really know what I mean when I say that there are bullies and bad characters among our own people, for no one is really "bad" deep down.

I should have liked to reach out to that man with all his fears, I should have liked to trace the source of his panic, to drive him ever deeper into himself; that is the only thing we can do, Klaas, in times like these.

And you, Klaas, give a tired and despondent wave and say, "But what you propose to do takes such a long time, and we don't really have all that much time, do we?" And I reply, "What you want is something people have been trying to get for the last two thousand years, and for many more thousand years before that, in fact, ever since mankind has existed on earth." "And what do you think the result has been, if I may ask?" you say.

And I repeat with the same old passion, although I am gradually beginning to think that I am being tiresome, "It is the only thing we can do, Klaas. I see no alternative: each of us must turn inward and destroy in himself all he thinks he ought to destroy in others. And remember that every atom of hate we add to this world makes it still more inhospitable. And you, Klaas, dogged old class fighter[15] that you have always been, dismayed and astonished at the same time, say, 'But that — that is nothing but Christianity!' "[16]

And I, amused by your confusion, retort quite coolly, "Yes, Christianity, and whyever not?"

— September 23, 1942, Wednesday

---

15. In reference to his activities and membership in the Dutch Communist Party and later in the Revolutionary-Socialist Labor Party until the late 1930s.

16. Referring to Jesus' saying: "You have heard that it was said, 'You shall love your neighbor and hate your enemy.' But I say to you, Love your enemies and pray for those who persecute you" (Matt. 5:43–44).

SURRENDER AND ACCEPTING DEATH

Despite fear and internal resistance, surrender to circumstances can mean a new birth and new life. Facing one's fear, rather than denying and fleeing from it, is a common theme in the writings of mystics and spiritual masters. Facing fear means its acceptance and acknowledgment and prepares one for the possibility of increased internal strength, clarity, and vision. Denying fear, fleeing from it, or circumventing it by blaming and accusing others for causing such fear means circumventing the possibility of internal clarity, vision, and strength; it also means compromising on the experience of life's fullness and its "blazing harmonies." On numerous occasions, Etty surrenders to the situation at hand and faces her fears, the fear of the ego's death, rather than avoiding or fleeing from them. She acknowledges her bouts with depression, submits to therapy, and experiences a spiritual rebirth. She acknowledges her dependence on Spier, surrenders to the opportunity of working for the Jewish Council despite mixed emotions about the agency, and gains a new freedom and a sense of inner strength. She accepts her longing and the gifts she has for being "a balm for all wounds," for rendering life to those whose soul had become "dead," for recovering "the sunken treasure" in them, submits to the conditions of hardship that such work entails, and gains closeness to God and people as a result. Each act of surrender and acceptance of death, the one witnessed in herself and others and the daily physical suffering and death at the camp, is made in the face of fear, the fear of spiritual or physical death, and it repeatedly demands from her the courage to entrust her life to God. Each time her courage is rewarded with a growing sense of intimacy with herself, with God, with others. In the end, she faces the fear of physical death. Rather than escaping deportation and leaving the camp when still possible

for her to do so, she insists on staying there to be with her
parents and brother.

"What is it in human beings that makes them want to destroy
others?" Jan asked bitterly.

I said, "Human beings, you say, but remember that you're
one yourself." And strangely enough he seemed to acquiesce,
grumpy, gruff old Jan. "The rottenness of others is in us, too," I
continued to preach at him. "I see no other solution, I really see
no other solution than to turn inward and to root out all the
rottenness there. I no longer believe that we can change anything in the world until we have first changed ourselves. And
that seems to me the only lesson to be learned from this war.
That we must look into ourselves and nowhere else."

. . . We stood there in the cold waiting for the tram, Jan with
his great purple chilblained hands and his toothache. Our professors are in prison, another of Jan's friends has been killed,
and there are so many other sorrows, but all we said to each
other was, "It is too easy to feel vindictive."

— February 19, 1942, Thursday, 2:00 p.m.

Yesterday I suddenly thought: there will always be suffering,
and whether one suffers from this or from that really doesn't
make much difference. It is the same with love. One should be
less and less concerned with the love object and more and more
with love itself, if it is to be real love. People may grieve more
for a cat that has been run over than for the countless victims
of a city that has been bombed out of existence. It is not the
object but the suffering, the love, the emotions, and the qual-
ity of these emotions that count. And the big emotions, those
basic harmonies, are always ablaze ("blazing harmonies" is not
bad!), and every century may stoke the fire with fresh fuels, but
all that matters is the warmth of the fire. And the fact that,
nowadays, we have yellow stars and concentration camps and

terror, and war is of secondary importance. And I don't feel less militant because of this attitude of mine, for moral integrity and moral indignation are also part of the "big emotions." But genuine moral indignation must run deep and not be petty personal hatred, for personal hatred usually means little more than using passing incidents as excuses for keeping alive personal hurts, perhaps suffered years ago.

— April 30, 1942, Thursday, after supper

Humiliation always involves two. The one who does the humiliating, and the one who allows himself to be humiliated. If the second is missing, that is, if the passive party is immune to humiliation, then the humiliation vanishes into thin air. All that remains are vexatious measures that interfere with daily life but are not humiliations that weigh heavily on the soul. We Jews should remember that. This morning I cycled along the Station Quay enjoying the broad sweep of the sky at the edge of the city and breathing in the fresh, unrationed air. And everywhere signs barring Jews from the paths and the open country. But above the one narrow path still left to us stretches the sky, intact. They can't do anything to us, they really can't. They can harass us, they can rob us of our material goods, of our freedom of movement, but we ourselves forfeit our greatest assets by our misguided compliance. By our feelings of being persecuted, humiliated, and oppressed. By our own hatred. By our swagger, which hides our fear. We may of course be sad and depressed by what has been done to us; that is only human and understandable. However, our greatest injury is one we inflict upon ourselves. I find life beautiful, and I feel free. The sky within me is as wide as the one stretching above my head. I believe in God and I believe in man, and I say so without embarrassment. Life is hard, but that is no bad thing. If one starts by taking one's own importance seriously, the rest follows. It is not morbid individualism to work on oneself. True peace will come only

when every individual finds peace within himself; when we have all vanquished and transformed our hatred of our fellow human beings of whatever race — even into love one day, although perhaps that is asking too much. It is, however, the only solution.
— June 20, 1942, Saturday night, 12:30 a.m.

When we are deprived of our lives, are we really deprived of very much? And I wonder if there is much of a difference between being consumed here by a thousand fears or in Poland by a thousand lice and by hunger? We have to accept death as part of life, even the most horrible of deaths.

And don't we live an entire life each one of our days, and does it really matter if we live a few days more or less? I am in Poland every day, on the battlefields, if that's what one can call them. I often see visions of poisonous green smoke; I am with the hungry, with the ill-treated and the dying, every day, but I am also with the jasmine and with that piece of sky beyond my window; there is room for everything in a single life. For belief in God and for a miserable end.
— July 2, 1942, Thursday, 7:30 a.m.

What they are after is our total destruction. I accept it. I know it now, and I shall not burden others with my fears. I shall not be bitter if others fail to grasp what is happening to us Jews. I work and continue to live with the same conviction, and I find life meaningful — yes, meaningful — although I hardly dare say so in company these days. Living and dying, sorrow and joy, the blisters on my feet and the jasmine behind the house, the persecution, the unspeakable horrors — it is all as one in me, and I accept it all as one mighty whole and begin to grasp it better if only for myself, without being able to explain to anyone else how it all hangs together. I wish I could live for a long time so that one day I may know how to explain it, and if I am not granted that wish, well, then somebody else will perhaps do it, carry on from where my life has been cut short. And that is why I must try to live a good and faithful life to my last breath: so that those who come after me do not have to start all over again, need not face the same difficulties. Isn't that doing something for future generations? Bernard's Jewish friend had them ask me after the latest promulgations, "Don't I now agree that all Germans should be done away with, preferably hung, drawn, and quartered?"

— July 3, 1942, Friday evening, 8:30 p.m.

I have come to terms with life. Nothing can happen to me, and after all my personal fate is not the issue; it doesn't really matter if it is I who perish or another. What matters is that we are all marked men. That's what I sometimes say to others, although it doesn't make much sense and doesn't really explain what I mean — and that doesn't really matter either. By "coming to terms with life" I mean: the reality of death has become a definite part of my life; my life has, so to speak, been extended by death, by my looking death in the eye and accepting it, by accepting destruction as part of life and no longer wasting my energies on fear of death or the refusal to acknowledge its inevitability. Through non-acceptance and through having all those fears, most people are left with just a pitiful and mutilated slice of life, which can hardly be called life at all. It sounds paradoxical: by excluding death from our life we cannot live a full life, and by admitting death into our life we enlarge and enrich it. — July 3, 1942, Friday

I feel so strange. Am I really sitting here writing things down so calmly? Would anybody understand me if I told them that I feel so strangely happy, not bursting with it, but just plain happy, because I can sense a new gentleness and a new confidence growing stronger inside me from day to day? That all the confusing and threatening and dreadful things that assail me do not drive me out of my mind for even one moment? Because I go on seeing and experiencing life in such plain and clear outlines. Because there is nothing that obscures my thinking and feeling. Because I can bear everything and cope with everything, and the realization that all the good in life, my own included, has not been superseded by everything else but keeps growing stronger in me. I hardly dare write on, I don't know how to put it, it is as if I had gone almost too far in my dissociation from all that drives most people out of their minds. If I knew for certain that I should die next week, I would still be able to sit at my desk all week and study with perfect equanimity, for I know now that life and death make a meaningful whole. Death is a gentle slipping away, even when gloom and abomination are its trappings.   —July 6, 1942, Monday, 11:00 a.m.

Well now, let's put a lid on all today's tumult, and I'll have this evening to myself in peace and quiet concentration. A yellow tea rose on my desk is flanked by two small vases of violets. After our "regular evening conversation" with the others, S. looked utterly worn out and said, "How on earth do the Levies stand it? I can't take any more; I feel absolutely awful." As for me, I am able to put everything, fact and rumor, behind me and study and read all evening. How odd: not a single one of the day's worries and alarms has followed me here; I sit at my desk "untouched," immersed in my studies as if nothing were happening in the world outside. Everything has simply fallen away from me, leaving no trace, and I feel more "receptive" than ever before. Next week no doubt it will be the turn of the Dutch Jews.[17] With each minute that passes I shed more

---

17. The medical examination and summons for deportation to Westerbork; to begin with, it was the German Jews that were being summoned in high numbers, four thousand a week, so that the Dutch Jews would soon be next.

wishes and desires and attachments. I am ready for everything, for anywhere on this earth, wherever God may send me, and I am ready to bear witness in any situation and unto death that life is beautiful and meaningful and that it is not God's fault that things are as they are at present, but our own. We have been granted every opportunity to enter every paradise, but we still have to learn to handle these opportunities. It is as if I shed further burdens from moment to moment, as if all the divisions there now are between men and nations are being removed for me. There are moments when I can see right through life and the human heart, when I understand more and more and become calmer and calmer and am filled with a faith in God that has grown so quickly inside me that it frightened me at first but has now become inseparable from me. And now to work. First some Jung, from *The Unconscious in Normal and Abnormal Psychology.* —July 7, 1942, Tuesday, 8:00 p.m.

Written while still on sick leave from Westerbork on the same day that Spier died; his death occurred at 7:15 a.m. Etty's permit of sick leave ran out on that day and was extended so she could attend Spier's funeral, where Tide sang. A longer prayer precedes this excerpt.

The tree is still there, the tree that could write my life story. But it is no longer the same tree; or is it I who am no longer the same? And there is the bookcase, within reach of my bed. I have only to stretch out my left hand to touch Dostoevsky or Shakespeare or Kierkegaard. But I do not stretch out my hand. I feel so dizzy. "You have placed me before Your ultimate mystery, oh God. I am grateful to You for that, I even have the strength to accept it and to know there is no answer. That we must be able to bear Your mysteries."

...Everything lives in me. I am reminded of a phrase in one of Rilke's poems: "outer space within."[18] And now I must sleep and let everything go. I am so dizzy. Nothing in my body feels right. I want so badly to get well again. "But I accept everything from Your hands, oh God, as it comes. I know that it is always good. I have discovered that by bearing one's heavy burden one can convert it into something good."

— September 15, 1942, Tuesday morning, 10:30 a.m.

Sometimes, when I least expect it, someone suddenly kneels down in some corner of my being. When I'm out walking or just talking to people. And that someone, the one who kneels down, is myself.

And now a mortal shell lies on that more than familiar bed. Oh, that cretonne coverlet! I hardly need to go back there again. It's all being played out somewhere inside me, everything; there are wide plains inside me beyond time and space, and everything is played out there. And now I walk along those few streets again. How often I have walked them with him, always engaged in absorbing and worthwhile dialogue. And how often will I be walking there again, no matter in what corner of the earth I happen to be? Am I expected to put on a sad or solemn face? I am not really sad, am I? I would like to fold my hands and say, "Friends, I am happy and grateful, and I find life very beautiful and meaningful. Yes, even as I stand here by the body of my dead companion, one who died much too soon, and just when I may be deported to some unknown destination. And yet, God, I am grateful for everything.

I shall live on with that part of the dead that lives forever, and I shall rekindle into life that of the living that is now dead, until there is nothing but life, one great life, oh God."

— September 16, 1942, Wednesday, 3:00 p.m.

---

18. See p. 79.

Tide told me that a girlfriend once said after the death of her husband, "God has moved me up into a more advanced class; the desks are still a little too big for me."

And when we spoke about his not being there anymore and how strange it was that neither of us felt empty inside, indeed had a sense of fulfillment, Tide simply ducked her head and shrugged her shoulders and said with a brave little laugh, "Yes, the desks are still a little too big; things are bound to be a bit difficult now and then."

Matthew 5:23–24: *Therefore if you bring thy gift to the altar, and there rememberest that thy brother hath ought against thee;* Leave there thy gift before the altar, and go thy way; *first be reconciled to thy brother, and then come and offer thy gift.*

Once in a while a treasure fleet is lost at sea, and mankind forever keeps trying to raise that sunken treasure from the waters. Many treasure fleets have already foundered in my heart, and I shall try all my life to bring some of the sunken treasure to the surface. I still lack the equipment, though, and shall have to assemble it from scratch.

I was hurrying along at Ru's side, and after a very long conversation in which we broached all the "ultimate questions" once again, I suddenly stopped beside him in the middle of the narrow, dreary Govert Flinck Straat, and said, "But you know, Ru, like a child I still feel that life is beautiful, and this helps me to bear everything." Ru looked at me full of expectation, and I said, as if it were the most ordinary thing in the world — and it really is, "Yes, you see, I believe in God." And, I think, he was rather taken aback, then, searching my face for some mysterious sign, appeared to like what he found there. Perhaps that is why I felt so radiant and so strong for the rest of the day? Because it came out so spontaneously and so simply in the middle of that drab working-class district, "Yes, you see, I believe in God."

I'm glad I've been able to stay on in Amsterdam for a few weeks. I am going back refreshed and reinvigorated. I used to

be much too unsociable, much too indolent. I really ought to
have gone to see those old people, the Bodenheimers, and not
have let myself off with the excuse that there's nothing I can
do for them. And there were so many other things like that
where I fell short. I pursued my own pleasure too much. I was
so ready, of an evening on the heath, to gaze into a friendly pair
of eyes. That was lovely, and yet I fell short in so many ways.
Even with the girls in my dormitory. From time to time I would
fling them a little piece of myself and then run away. It was
not nearly good enough. And yet I am thankful it was like that
and that I shall be able to make amends when I get back. I'm
sure I'll be returning in a more serious and more concentrated
frame of mind, less in pursuit of my own pleasure. If one wants
to exert a moral influence on others, one must start with one's
own morals. I keep talking about God the whole day long, and
it is high time that I lived accordingly. I still have a long way to
go, oh yes, a long way, and yet sometimes I behave as if I were
there already. I am frivolous and easygoing, and I often look on
things that happen as if I were an artist, a mere observer. There
is something bizarre and fickle and adventurous in me. But as
I sit here at my desk, late at night, I also feel a compelling,
directive force deep down, a great and growing seriousness, a
soundless voice that tells me what to do and forces me to con-
fess: I have fallen short in all ways; my real work has not even
begun. So far I have done little more than play about.

—September 25, 1942, Friday, 11:00 p.m.

It made quite an impression on me that time, when that flirt
of a doctor with his melancholy eyes said to me, "You live too
cerebral a life, it's bad for your health, your constitution isn't
up to it." When I told Jopie about it, he said reflectively, "He's
probably right."

I worried about it for quite a long time, but then I realized
with ever-greater certainty: he wasn't right. True, I may think

too much, sometimes with a demonic and ecstatic intensity, but I refresh myself from day to day at the original source, life itself, and I rest from time to time in prayer. And what those who say "You live too intensely" do not know is that one can withdraw into a prayer as into a convent cell and leave again with renewed strength and with peace regained.

I think what weakens people most is fear of wasting their strength. If after a long and arduous process, day in, day out, you manage to come to grips with your inner sources, with God, in short, and if only you make certain that your path to God is unblocked — which you can do by "working on yourself" — then you can keep renewing yourself at these inner sources and need never again be afraid of wasting your strength.

I do not believe in objective statements. There is an unending combination of human interactions.

People say that you died too young. Well, one book less on psychology may get written, but you have brought a little more love into the world. — September 28, 1942, Monday

After a brief descriptive account of life at the camp, people, barracks, transports, the death of children, conversations with colleagues, workers, relatives, old acquaintances who had been brought to the camp and who with hesitation and shudders shared with one another the strain of what they had witnessed:

And that's why I don't like to write about it, either. But I am digressing. All I wanted to say is this: The misery here is quite terrible; and yet, late at night when the day has slunk away into the depths behind me, I often walk with a spring in my step along the barbed wire. And then, time and again, it soars straight from my heart — I can't help it, that's just the way it is, like some elementary force — the feeling that life is glorious and magnificent, and that one day we shall be building a whole new world. Against every new outrage and every fresh horror, we shall put up one more piece of love and goodness, drawing strength from within ourselves. We may suffer, but we must not succumb. And if we should survive unhurt in body and soul, but above all in soul, without bitterness and without hatred, then we shall have a right to a say after the war. Maybe I am an ambitious woman: I would like to have just a tiny little bit of a say.

You speak about suicide,[19] and about mothers and children. Yes, I know what you mean, but I find it a morbid subject. There is a limit to suffering; perhaps no human being is given more to bear than he can shoulder; beyond a certain point we just die. People are dying here even now of a broken spirit, because they can no longer find any meaning in life, young people. The old ones are rooted in firmer soil and accept their fate with dignity and calm. You see so many different sorts of people here, and so many different attitudes to the hardest, the ultimate questions. . . .

I shall try to convey to you how I feel, but am not sure if my metaphor is right. When a spider spins its web, does it not cast the main threads ahead of itself; and then follow along them from behind? The main path of my life stretches like a long journey before me and already reaches into another world. It is just as if everything that happens here and that is still to happen were somehow discounted inside me. As if I had been through it already, and was now helping to build a new and different society. Life here hardly touches my deepest resources — physically, perhaps, you do decline a little, and sometimes you are infinitely sad — but fundamentally you keep growing stronger. I just hope that it can be the same for you and all my friends. We need it, for we still have so much to experience together and so much

---

19. Directed at Klaas Smelik, who had once ordered his daughter, Johanna, to bring him poison so he could commit suicide; when she refused, he lost his temper and beat her. Etty was present and ran for help, drumming up neighbors and the police.

work to do. And so I call upon you: stay at your inner post, and please do not feel sorry or sad for me, there is no reason to.

— From Letter #46 to Johanna and Klaas Smelik and others, Westerbork, Saturday, July 3, 1943,

FINDING GOD IN ALL THINGS

The theme of "finding God in all things" is commonly associated with the sixteenth-century priest, monk, and mystic Ignatius of Loyola (1491–1556), founder of the Society of Jesus, the Jesuit order. For Ignatius, God could be found not only in worship and private devotion but also in daily activity, in the things of the world, in the smallest detail in nature and work, in the daily encounter with people. Ignatius came to this insight through the daily practice of prayer in solitude, daily celebration of the Eucharist (by himself), simplicity of speech and lifestyle in a semi-monastic setting, daily examination of conscience, discipline in organizing the work of the order and carrying on a vast correspondence, and the firm belief that whatever was set before him was part of God's design. Obstacles, intrigue, enemies, and detractors each could teach him to rely on God more and hence were part of God's world and his redeeming measures. In the twentieth century, two Jesuit priests stand out for this type of mysticism: Teilhard de Chardin, S.J. (1881–1955), a paleontologist who saw God's activity present in matter as well as in spirit-filled creatures, thus regarding matter and spirit as two cosmic complementary movements of the same God whose manifestation he described as "the spirit of fire"; and Karl Rahner, S.J. (1904–84), one of the greatest theologians of the twentieth century and often referred to as a "mystic of everyday life," due to his writings on God's grace as active and at work everywhere in the world and God's mysterious self-communication being available to all people everywhere, not just in sacred settings but in daily life and the routines of work, sitting, sleeping, walking, or eating. Etty, too, finds God at work and present in all things. By her daily prayer practice, her continuous internal dialogue with God, her discipline in "being true to herself," and the examination of her conscience and her soul, she develops an interior reality, an interior world, that allows her to see God's presence and activity in all things of the world. The deeper she feels inwardly connected and grounded, the closer she senses her interconnectedness with the outside world. Whether at work or at rest, whether with a circle of friends or among strangers, whether in the things of nature or in the gestures and faces of people, she is aware of the spirit within and the "fire" that illuminates and permeates her and helps her see the world in a colorful new light, one steeped in God's love. All things are worthy of her attention and love and allow her to feel at one with God, regardless of where she is and what the circumstances. This sense of at-oneness with herself and the world, the continuity between the past and the present, the interconnectedness of all aspects of creation and life, give her boundless joy and hope and make her declare repeatedly that life is meaningful and God good.

The small red buds and the tiny white ones, so tight, so inaccessible, so incredibly dear — I had them to look at all afternoon, while listening to Hugo Wolf.[20] The Rijksmuseum, too, was there outside the window, so invitingly fresh and new in its contours and at the same time so old and familiar. We are not allowed to walk along the Promenade any longer, and every miserable little clump of two or three trees has been pronounced a wood with a board nailed up: No admittance to Jews. More and more of these boards are appearing all over the place. Nevertheless there is still enough room for one to move and live

---

20. Hugo Wolf (1860–1903) was a German composer, who wrote many romantic songs.

and be happy and play music and love each other. Glassner[21] brought a little sack of coal and Tide some wood, S. sugar and biscuits, I had some tea, and our small Swiss vegetarian artist suddenly arrived with a big cake. First S. read to us about Hugo Wolf. And when he came to some passages about Wolf's tragic life, his mouth quivered a little. That's another reason why I love him so much. He is so genuine. And lives every word he says or sings or reads. When he reads sad things, he is genuinely sad. And I am touched by the fact that at that moment he looks as if he is about to burst into tears. And I would gladly weep in unison with him.

Glassner gets better and better at the piano. This afternoon I said to him privately, "We are with you as you grow, dear quiet Glassner." — March 22, 1942, Sunday morning, 8:30 a.m.

While reading some letters with S.

. . . a slice of the past, of 1933, came unexpectedly bobbing up to the surface again. I can scarcely believe I went through all that, or rather I can believe it only too well — everything I have ever experienced has remained with me and lies at rest deep within me, assimilated and in good shape, and that is perhaps why I feel so satisfied, so rich, so replete, so filled with experience.

But that sense of satisfaction does not make me long for new adventures, and because I am no longer in such a state of agitation, life has turned into one great, unpredictable, continuous inner adventure, and every minute of the day and night, as it were, provides fuel for that adventure. And nowadays I get a bit of a rest as well: sometimes between two deep breaths

21. Evaristos Edgar Glassner (1912–88) was a German church organist and pianist; he had graduated in organ from the Conservatory in Berlin and worked as an organist in a Protestant church in Germany. No longer allowed to play there for being Jewish, he moved to Amsterdam in 1937 and became the house pianist at the musical gatherings of the "Spier club," accompanying Spier, Tide, and Adri Holm, who sang songs by Schubert, Mahler, and Brahms.

and sometimes by kneeling for five minutes, anywhere I may find myself in the house. And whatever I experience, however emotional it may be, I assimilate on the spot and at the time.

That does not mean that I forget the experience there and then, but that I fit it directly, irresistibly, into the greater current of my life; it flows, as it were, with the great stream and no longer sets up, as it used to do, barriers and dams and impurities blocking the great stream of life. I still have to tell Leonie that she knows more about the countless small waves than about the big stream, the one great wave which absorbs all the little waves. And that she needs to gain a better understanding of that one great stream.

So this is my attitude to life at the moment: it flows through me as a great, rich, mighty river, fed by an infinite number of small tributaries — etc.

— March 27, 1942, Friday morning, 10:30 a.m.

I am feeling so strange: so peaceful and earnest and resolute, and so filled with serious yet cheerful life. At this moment I know, more certainly than ever, that I have a task in this life, a small project especially for me. And I shall have to live through everything. I am grateful that fate has not got me in one of its small clutches — for instance, in prison for hiding silver, yes, that sort of thing happens — but that I shall be swept away with the great stream. I shall become the chronicler of our adventures. I shall forge them into a new language and store them inside me should I have no chance to write things down. I shall grow dull and come to life again, fall down and rise up again, and one day I may perhaps discover a peaceful space round me that is mine alone, and then I shall sit there for as long as it takes, even if it should be a year, until life begins to bubble up in me again and I find the words that bear witness where witness needs to be borne....

... life remains so "interesting" through it all. Ever-present in me is an almost demonic urge to watch everything that happens. A wish to see and to hear and to be present, to worm out all of life's secrets, to observe with detachment what people look like in their last convulsions. And also, suddenly, to be forced to face oneself and to learn what one can from the spectacle that one's own soul enacts in these times. And later to be able to find the right words for it.

I shall read through my old diaries. I have decided not to tear them up after all. Perhaps later on they will help reacquaint me with my former self.

We have had more than enough time to prepare for our present catastrophe: two whole years. And the last of these has proved to be the most crucial of my life, my most beautiful year. And I know for certain that there will be a continuity between the life I have led and the life about to begin. Because my life is increasingly an inner one, and the outer matters less and less.

— July 28, 1942, Tuesday, afternoon and evening

Rilke. I am reading his letters now. Each and every day he discovered a few good, precious, original words for nature, for various people. Every day, so to speak, he discovered new endearments and friendly gestures, for the air, for the rain, for the sun, for "things." And in the last analysis he was not the man to sit about wringing his hands over little flowers and birds, he was always working, and hard at work what is more. And why shouldn't we find a few fresh words and endearments every day for the everyday things around us and for the air we breathe? ...

A longing for silence. As it is, silence has come back to me, and I carry it within me all the time. I have something I must tell Liesl, who says that she feels happy only in nature. One has to carry Nature within one; one can experience it in a flower, in a cloud, in a feeling in one's own blood. One can gather it all up into oneself and carry it inside. That can be done. But going after things cannot always be done. Nor ought one to grow dependent on them.

— April 13, 1942, Monday morning, 8:30 a.m.

During a walk with S. on a country road on Easter Monday.

A small brook, willows and meadows and in the distance the town. And his gesticulating hands and expressive head. And during our walk we passed a long, low-built house that came from a different century, and the house had a sad face of its own and it reached out to me. What I mean is that I felt in touch with everything round me, at one with the landscape through which I was walking, and with an old house that suddenly came alive for me. Rilke. The "Things...."[22]

Well, that Monday, that Easter Monday. Liesl and Werner at two o'clock in the morning, like two Parisian street urchins sitting on the edge of their improvised gypsy beds in the living room. And me in Renate's bed.[23] I took the blackout paper down from the window, and suddenly there were two stars at the head of the bed. They were not the same stars I see through my window, but I felt in touch with them all the same, and suddenly I was quite certain that no matter where I was in the world I would always find stars and be able to flop down on a bed, or on a floor, or anywhere else, and feel absolutely at home.

And of this rich, oh, so rich Easter Monday, these were probably the two things that mattered most of all: the house that

---

22. "Things" are a frequent theme of Rilke; they can denote the things in nature, animals, and inanimate objects, such as the sun, the stars, clouds, the sky, water, trees, stones, representing what has no voice of its own and is dependent on human compassion for love and appreciation. "Things" are also a reflection of all that is pure, essential, unadulterated, and undefiled by grasping human hands, hence representative of the essence or core of life, life's soul, God.

23. Renate was the older daughter of the Levies, and Etty spent the night at their place on occasion.

reached out to me and showed me its face, and those two stars at two o'clock in the morning at the head of Renate's narrow child's bed.   —April 16, 1942, Thursday, 9:00 a.m.

By my faded hyacinth out on the veranda:
   Some time ago I wrote to him, "One must not divide one's single great desire into a hundred small satisfactions." And now I want to add: one must divide one's single great tenderness into a thousand small tendernesses, lest one succumb to the weight of that one great tenderness. A thousand small tendernesses: for a dog in the road, or for an old flower seller — and finding the right word for someone in need. And also not feeling sad because one imagines one cannot express that single, great, strong feeling one carries inside. On Friday night, when I cycled back from his rooms through the spring night, I poured the great love and overwhelming tenderness I feel for him into the night, put some of it into the stars and left some behind in the bushes beside the canal. And this too: one must also be able to wear and to bear, to tolerate and endure, one's own strong feelings. One must not keep wanting to be rid of them but must be able to carry them round with one, and not be crushed by them but draw strength from them, not just for one man but for so many of God's creatures which also have a right to our attention and love.   —April 26, 1942, Sunday, 9:00 p.m.

Last night I laid the breakfast table in advance and set my alarm for seven o'clock. Bright and early, I found myself in the company of St. Augustine and want to hold on to a few words of his. Always the same thing, in nuances and tonalities that are ever-changing but always the same:

> My soul shall praise Thee in all things, God, Creator of the Universe, but it shall not cling to them in sinful love with the senses of the body. For everything goes to where

it has always gone, and ceases to be; and our soul is torn
with sick desires, for it wants to be and rest with the things
it loves. In them, however, there is no resting, for they do
not last. They depart, and who can follow them with the
senses of the flesh, even when they lie before him? For
slow are the senses of the flesh, and who can grasp them
even when they lie before him? For slow are the senses of
the flesh.[24]

The bare trunks that climb past my window now shelter under a
cover of young green leaves. A springy fleece along their naked,
though, ascetic limbs.

Well, how was it last night in my small bedroom? I went to
bed early last night, and from my bed I stared out through the
large open window. And it was once more as if life with all
its mysteries was close to me, as if I could touch it. I had the
feeling that I was resting against the naked breast of life and
could feel her gentle and regular heartbeat. I felt safe and protected. And I thought, How strange. It is wartime. There are
concentration camps. Small barbarity mounts upon small barbarity. I can say of so many of the houses I pass: here the son
has been thrown into prison, there the father has been taken
hostage, and an eighteen-year-old boy in that house over there
has been sentenced to death. And these streets and houses are
all so close to my own. I know how very nervous people are;
I know about the mounting human suffering. I know the persecution and oppression and despotism and the impotent fury
and the terrible sadism. I know it all and continue to confront
every shred of reality that thrusts itself upon me. And yet — at

---

24. Quoted from St. Augustine, *Confessions*; St. Augustine (354–430) was
bishop of Hippo in the Roman province of North Africa. Of his extensive body
of writings, the *Confessions* is his most personal work. Written as an honest confession of sin and a bold profession of personal faith, this autobiographical work
resembles a long hymn of praise and a love letter to God. In reading St. Augustine,
Etty says that the only love letters one ought to write are love letters to God.

unguarded moments, when left to myself, I suddenly lie against the naked breast of life, and her arms round me are so gentle and so protective, and my own heartbeat is difficult to describe: so slow and so regular and so soft, almost muffled, but so constant, as if it would never stop, and so good and merciful as well.

That is my attitude to life, and I believe that neither war nor any other senseless human atrocity will ever be able to change it.

— May 30, 1942, Saturday morning, 7:30 a.m.

It seems to be such a small thing, but it takes a great deal of struggle and self-education to go on from the theory of self-discipline and training to daily practice. For instance, taking leave of the day at night without too much resistance, instead of spending hours leafing through all sorts of books or running about the house from sheer restlessness and dissatisfaction with the day's achievements. In the past that used to happen a lot. I kept hoping until the very last moment then for the miracle that would turn the day into something special. A kind of P.S., containing everything that had been lacking during the main part. It's not so bad any longer, except just now and then. In the past the transitions used to be much more of a shock to me: from day to night, from working to doing nothing, from being alone to being with others — they were all so abrupt. Now everything merges more smoothly because an internal rhythm has emerged, a rhythm that is mine and mine alone.

It may seem exaggerated, but it is quite true: to go to bed on time, to let go of the day voluntarily, requires discipline. One has first to have it brought home to one before it happens automatically and becomes part of one's life rhythm. . . .

Relaxing one's rigid grip on the day. I think many people keep hanging on to a portion of the day with their greedy, grasping claws even at night. There must be an act of surrender and release every evening: a letting go of the day, and of

everything that has happened in it. And a letting go of everything one has not brought to a satisfactory conclusion during
the day, in the knowledge that there will be another. One must,
so to speak, enter the night with empty, open hands from which
one has deliberately allowed the day to slip. For only then can
one have a good rest. And into one's rested and empty hands,
which are no longer trying to cling to anything and from which
all desire has gone, one receives a new day upon awakening.

Isn't my new day sometimes tainted with qualities inherited
from the previous day? And can't a new day sometimes find
it hard to get going, half buried as it is under the rubble and
refuse of the one before?

—June 17, 1942, Wednesday morning, 7:30 a.m.

Like a strong, vigorous tree shedding a withered leaf, so I too
can sometimes let go of people who are close to me with a
shrug of near indifference and boredom.... "I have the best life
of anyone in Europe and Asia," I confided to S. on his sunny
gravel roof this afternoon. And I meant it. I wouldn't want to
change with anyone. But I must always remember that I live a
privileged life. I am a loner, and I can fly as high and as fast
as I like. I am only at the beginning, but the beginning is there,
that much I know for certain. It means gathering together all
the strength one can, living one's life with God and in God and
having God dwell within.

—June 22, 1942, Monday night, 9:00 p.m.

God is not accountable to us, but we are to Him. I know what
may lie in wait for us. Even now I am cut off from my parents and cannot reach them, although they are only two hours
away by train. But I know exactly where they are, and that
they're not going short of food, and that there are many kind
people all round them. And they know where I am, too. But I
am also aware that there may come a time when I shan't know

where they are, when they might be deported to perish miserably in some unknown place. I know this is perfectly possible. The latest news is that all Jews will be transported out of Holland through Drenthe Province and then on to Poland. And the English radio has reported that seven hundred thousand Jews perished last year alone, in Germany and the occupied territories. And even if we stay alive, we shall carry the wounds with us throughout our lives.

And yet I don't think life is meaningless. And God is not accountable to us for the senseless harm we cause one another. We are accountable to Him! I have already died a thousand deaths in a thousand concentration camps. I know about everything and am no longer appalled by the latest reports. In one way or another I know it all. And yet I find life beautiful and meaningful. From minute to minute.

—June 29, 1942, Monday morning, 10:00 a.m.

Upon reflecting on

... my sudden irritation and aggressiveness towards Käthe when I feel that deep down she is defending her country, or rather, the good there is in her country, for, after all, those who live there are people like ourselves. Surely that is right? You can spin as many theories as you like, but they are people like ourselves. That is something we must cling to through thick and thin, and shout in the face of all that hatred.

Yes, we carry everything within us, God and Heaven and Hell and Earth and Life and Death and all of history. The externals are simply so many props; everything we need is within us. And we have to take everything that comes: the bad with the good, which does not mean we cannot devote our life to curing the bad. But we must know what motives inspire our struggle, and we must begin with ourselves, every day anew.

—July 3, 1942, Friday

After a tiring walk with S. to and from the tax office:

And when at one point I was overcome with tiredness and had this sudden peculiar feeling about not being allowed to take a tram anywhere in this great city with its long streets, and not even being allowed to sit down at one of the little pavement cafés (I could tell him something about so many pavement cafés: "Look, that's where I went with my friends two years ago, after I took my finals"), then I thought, or rather I didn't really think it, it welled up somewhere inside me: throughout the ages people have been tired and have worn their feet out on God's earth, in the cold and the heat, and that, too, is part of life. This sort of feeling has been growing much stronger in me: a hint of eternity steals through my smallest daily activities and perceptions. I am not alone in my tiredness or sickness or fears, but at one with millions of others from many centuries, and it is all part of life, and yet life is beautiful and meaningful too. It is meaningful even in its meaninglessness, provided one makes room in one's life for everything, and accepts life as one indivisible whole, for then one becomes whole in oneself. But as soon as one tries to exclude certain parts of life, refusing to accept them and arrogantly opting for this and not that part of life, yes, then it does become meaningless because it is no longer a whole, and everything then becomes quite arbitrary.

—July 4, 1942, Saturday morning, 9:00 a.m.

My red and yellow roses are now fully open. While I sat there working in that hell, they quietly went on blooming. Many say, "How can you still think of flowers!"

Last night, walking that long way home through the rain with the blister on my foot, I still made a short detour to seek out a flower stall and went home with a large bunch of roses. And there they are. They are just as real as all the misery I witness each day. "There is room for many things in my life, so much room, oh God."

As I walked down those overcrowded corridors today, I suddenly felt the urge to kneel down right there, on the stone floor, among all those people. The only adequate gesture left to us in these times: "kneeling down before You."

Each day I learn something new about people and realize more and more that the only strength comes, not from others, but from within.

— July 23, 1942, Thursday evening, 9:00 p.m.

I often used to think to myself as I walked about in Westerbork among the noisily bickering, all too energetic members of the Jewish Council: if only I could enter a small piece of their soul. If only I could be the receptacle of their better nature, which is sure to be present in all of them. Let me *be* rather than *do*. Let me be the soul in that body. And I would now and then discover in each one of them a gesture or a glance that took them out of themselves and of which they seemed barely aware. And I felt I was the guardian of that gesture or glance.

— September 16, 1942, Wednesday morning, 9:00 a.m.
(in the doctor's waiting room)

I would love to be like the lilies of the field.[25] Someone who managed to read this age correctly would surely have learned just this: to be like a lily of the field.

I once wrote in one of my diaries, "I would like to run my fingertips along the contours of these times." I was sitting at my desk with no idea what to make of life. That was because I had not yet arrived at the life in myself, was still sitting at this desk. And then I was suddenly flung into one of many flash-points of human suffering. And there, in the faces of people, in a thousand gestures, small changes of expression, life stories, I was suddenly able to read our age — and much more than our

---

25. Reference to Matthew 6:28.

age alone. And then it suddenly happened: I was able to feel the contours of these times with my fingertips. How is it that this stretch of heathland surrounded by barbed wire, through which so much human misery has flooded, nevertheless remains inscribed in my memory as something almost lovely? How is it that my spirit, far from being oppressed, seemed to grow lighter and brighter there? It is because I read the signs of the times, and they did not seem meaningless to me. Surrounded by my writers and poets and the flowers on my desk, I loved life. And there among the barracks, full of hunted and persecuted people, I found confirmation of my love of life. Life in those drafty barracks was no other than life in this protected, peaceful room. Not for one moment was I cut off from the life I was said to have left behind. There was simply one great, meaningful whole. Will I be able to describe all that one day? So that others can feel too how lovely and worth living and just — yes, just — life really is? Perhaps one day God will give me the few simple words I need. And bright and fervent and serious words as well. But above all simple words. How can I draw this small village of barracks between heath and sky with a few rapid, delicate, and yet powerful strokes of the pen? And how can I let others see the many inmates, who have to be deciphered like hieroglyphs, stroke by stroke, until they finally form one great readable and comprehensible whole?

One thing I now know for certain: I shall never be able to put down in writing what life itself has spelled out for me in living letters. I have read it all, with my own eyes, and felt it with many senses. I shall never be able to repeat it. It would be enough to make me despair had I not learned to accept that one must work with the inadequate powers one has been given — but that one must really work with them.

I walk past people as if they were plants under cultivation, taking note how tall the crop of mankind has grown.

This house, I feel, is slowly losing its hold on me. It's a good thing to be able to cut all ties with it. Very carefully, with great sorrow, but also in the certainty that it is all for the best and that there can be no other way, I let go, day by day.

And with one shirt on my back and another in my rucksack … and with a very small Bible, perhaps my Russian dictionary and Tolstoy's folk tales, and no doubt, no doubt at all, there will be room for one volume of Rilke's letters. And then the lambswool sweater, knitted by a friend — what a lot of possessions I have, oh God, and someone like me wants to be a lily of the field! And with that one shirt in my rucksack I am off to an "unknown destination." That's what they call it. But wherever I go, won't there be the same earth under my roving feet and the same sky with now the moon and now the sun, not to mention all the stars, above my grateful head? So why speak of an unknown destination?   — September 22, 1942, Tuesday

At night the barracks sometimes lay in the moonlight, made out of silver and eternity: like a plaything that had slipped from God's preoccupied hand.   — September 23, Wednesday

To think that one can be such a fire, with such showers of sparks. All the words and all the expressions I once used to describe that seem gray and pale and colorless in comparison with the intense joy and love of life and vitality that is pouring from me right now.

My piano-playing little brother[26] aged twenty-one wrote this from a mental institution in the how-manieth? year of the war:

---

26. By then, Mischa Hillesum was widely known for his talents as a pianist and had been given certain privileges by the Nazi regime, which, at least temporarily, extended to his parents; when they were due to be transported to Westerbork, he insisted on joining them. All three arrived in Westerbork on June 21, 1943. Of the thousands of people shipped in that day, they were spotted by Etty while still on the train: she had glimpsed her mother's hat, her father's glasses, and Mischa's face peering through a small opening high up where the planks of the freight car were broken.

"Henny (*meaning Tide*), I too believe — I know — that there is another life after this one. I even believe that some people can see and experience that life together with this one. It is a world in which the eternal whispers of mystics have been made living reality, and in which common, everyday subjects or sayings have taken on a higher meaning. It is quite possible that after the war people will be more open to that world than they used to be, that they will collectively wake up to a higher world order."   — September 27, 1942, Sunday

Right now I've washed, written a letter I thought I needed to write, done the rounds of the house and cleaned my little room up a bit, and now, God, to put it very tritely, now I shall go to Your till and exchange all that heavy, jingling small change I carry round for a single blank banknote. What do You think of so much poetry on an empty stomach? But I am about to trade in all my many small worries for one great peace.

My parents, dear God, my parents! Of course, it is our complete destruction they want! But let us bear it with grace —

There is no hidden poet in me, just a little piece of God that might grow into poetry. And a camp needs a poet, one who experiences life there, even there, as a bard and is able to sing about it.

At night, as I lay in the camp on my plank bed, surrounded by women and girls gently snoring, dreaming aloud, quietly sobbing, and tossing and turning, women and girls who often told me during the day, "We don't want to think, we don't want to feel, otherwise we are sure to go out of our minds." I was sometimes filled with an infinite tenderness, and lay awake for hours letting all the many, too many impressions of a much-too-long day wash over me, and I prayed, "Let me be the thinking heart of these barracks." And that is what I want to be again. The thinking heart of a whole concentration camp. I lie here so patiently and now so calmly again that I feel quite a bit better already, not pretend better, but really better. I'm reading Rilke's letters *On God*,[27] every word is filled with meaning for me, I might have written them myself, and if I had then I would have wanted to write them just like that and no other way.

I feel my strength returning to me; I have stopped making plans and worrying about risks. Happen what may, it is bound to be for the good.

"Christ may have been right when, in an age filled with stale and threadbare gods, he spoke ill of earthly things, although (I cannot help thinking) it is slighting God not to see perfection and something to gladden us to the limit of our senses in all that has been granted us and bestowed upon us, if only we use it with meticulous care. The proper use, that is the thing. To seize what is to hand on earth, with heartfelt love, with amazement, as all we have for the time being: that, to put it plainly, is God's great directive, the one St. Francis meant to record in his song to the sun, which, as he lay dying, he thought more glorious than the Cross that, after all, just stood there *pointing* to the sun."[28]

— October 3, 1942, Saturday morning

I am still sick. I can do nothing about it. I shall have to wait a little longer to gather up all their tears and fears. Though I can really do it here just as well, here in bed. Perhaps that's why I feel so giddy and hot. I don't want to become a chronicler of horrors. Or of sensations. This morning I said to Jopie, "It still all comes down to the same thing: life is beautiful. And I believe in God. And I want to be there right in the thick of what people call 'horror' and still be able to say: life is beautiful." And now here I lie in some corner, dizzy and feverish and unable to do a thing. When I woke up just now I was parched, reached for my glass of water, and, grateful for that one sip, thought to

---

27. Referring to Rilke, *Über Gott. Zwei Briefe.*
28. Quote from Rilke's letters *On God*.

myself, "If I could only be there to give some of those parched thousands just one sip of water."

And all the time I keep telling myself, "Don't worry, things aren't all that bad." Whenever yet another poor woman broke down at one of our registration tables, or a hungry child started crying, I would go over to them and stand beside them protectively, arms folded across my chest, force a smile for those huddled, shattered scraps of humanity, and tell myself, "Things aren't all that bad, they really aren't that bad." And all I did was just stand there, for what else could one do? Sometimes I might sit down beside someone, put an arm round a shoulder, say very little and just look into their eyes. Nothing was alien to me, not one single expression of human sorrow. Everything seemed so familiar, as if I knew it all and had gone through it all before. People said to me, "You must have nerves of steel to stand up to it." I don't think I have nerves of steel, far from it, but I can certainly "stand up to things." I am not afraid to look suffering straight in the eyes.

And at the end of each day, there was always the feeling: I love people so much. Never any bitterness about what was done to them, but always love for those who knew how to bear so much although nothing had prepared them for such burdens.

— October 2, 1942, Thursday afternoon

Through me course wide rivers and in me rise tall mountains. And beyond the thickets of my agitation and confusion there stretch the wide plains of my peace and surrender. All landscapes are within me. And there is room for everything. The earth is in me, and the sky. And I well know that something like hell can also be in one, though I no longer experience it in myself, but I can still feel it in others with great intensity. And that is as it should be, or else I might grow too complacent.

— October 9, 1942, Next day

Etty's last lines, written on a postcard and thrown from the freight train on which she, her parents, and brother Mischa were being transported to Auschwitz.[29]

Christine, opening the Bible at random I find this: "The Lord is my tower."[30] I am sitting on my rucksack in the middle of a full freight car. Father, Mother, and Mischa are a few cars away. In the end, the departure came without warning. On sudden special orders from The Hague. We left the camp singing, Father and Mother firmly and calmly, Mischa, too. We shall be traveling for three days. Thank you for all your kindness and care. Friends left behind will still be writing to Amsterdam; perhaps you will hear something from them. Or from my last long letter from camp.[31]

Good-bye for now from the four of us.

Etty

— Letter #71 to Christine van Nooten,[32]
Near Glimmen, September 7, 1943, Tuesday

---

29. On the train were a total of 987 people, including 170 children; 8 people survived.

30. Possibly alluding to Psalm 18:3.

31. This letter was probably the one written on August 24, 1943; it is Letter #64 in the 2002 edition.

32. Christine van Nooten (1903–98) was one of Etty's Latin-Greek teachers, a colleague of Etty's father at the Deventer gymnasium, and later a friend of the family. When the Hillesums were deported to Camp Westerbork, van Nooten was one of their trusted contacts outside and regularly sent food parcels.

MODERN SPIRITUAL MASTERS
Robert Ellsberg, Series Editor

Already published:

Dietrich Bonhoeffer (edited by Robert Coles)
Simone Weil (edited by Eric O. Springsted)
Henri Nouwen (edited by Robert A. Jonas)
Pierre Teilhard de Chardin (edited by Ursula King)
Anthony de Mello (edited by William Dych, S.J.)
Charles de Foucauld (edited by Robert Ellsberg)
Oscar Romero (by Marie Dennis, Rennie Golden,
    and Scott Wright)
Eberhard Arnold (edited by Johann Christoph Arnold)
Thomas Merton (edited by Christine M. Bochen)
Thich Nhat Hanh (edited by Robert Ellsberg)
Rufus Jones (edited by Kerry Walters)
Mother Teresa (edited by Jean Maalouf)
Edith Stein (edited by John Sullivan, O.C.D.)
John Main (edited by Laurence Freeman)
Mohandas Gandhi (edited by John Dear)
Mother Maria Skobtsova (introduction by Jim Forest)
Evelyn Underhill (edited by Emilie Griffin)
St. Thérèse of Lisieux (edited by Mary Frohlich)
Flannery O'Connor (edited by Robert Ellsberg)
Clarence Jordan (edited by Joyce Hollyday)
G. K. Chesterton (edited by William Griffin)
Alfred Delp, S.J. (introduction by Thomas Merton)
Bede Griffiths (edited by Thomas Matus)
Karl Rahner (edited by Philip Endean)
Sadhu Sundar Singh (edited by Charles E. Moore)
Pedro Arrupe (edited by Kevin F. Burke, S.J.)

Romano Guardini (edited by Robert A. Krieg)
Albert Schweitzer (edited by James Brabazon)
Caryll Houselander (edited by Wendy M. Wright)
Brother Roger of Taizé (edited by Marcello Fidanzio)
Dorothee Soelle (edited by Dianne L. Oliver)
Leo Tolstoy (edited by Charles E. Moore)
Howard Thurman (edited by Luther E. Smith, Jr.)
Swami Abhishiktananda (edited by Shirley du Boulay)
Carlo Carretto (edited by Robert Ellsberg)
John XXIII (edited by Jean Maalouf)
Jean Vanier (edited by Carolyn Whitney-Brown)
The Dalai Lama (edited by Thomas A. Forsthoefel)
Catherine de Hueck Doherty (edited by David Meconi, S.J.)
Dom Helder Camara (edited by Francis McDonagh)

Made in the USA
Monee, IL
05 February 2021